Rebel Without A Pause Button
How I Became A Video Game Journalist

by Torrence Davis

Edited By
Wendy Alcindor

Table Of Contents

Dedication

Dedicated to Perry Mercer who was right there at the beginning of this ride. He was the truest gamer I've ever known and he stayed true to the very end.

In The Beginning

I can remember back in the 70's when arcades were packed with nothing but pinball machines. This was always amazing to me. Wall to wall lights, sounds and colors. Whether it was at MIT's popular arcade or at some fairgrounds, I always gravitated to these machines. Before I knew it, I was playing games like Pong and Space Invaders in addition to the pinball machines. Before I could absorb everything that was happening back then, arcades were completely stacked with video games. Pinball machines were moved to the back of the arcades and there weren't more than two or three of these machines. Sometimes an amazing pinball machine would arrive that encompassed a screen with mini-games. This would get some attention for a short period of time but for the most part, people were looking to get their digital fix on.

I was always eager to put quarters in video games. Whether it was at the local arcade or in a sub shop, if there was an arcade cabinet, I was in front of it. My fondest memories of video game arcade machines were with the Atari classics like Asteroids, Missile Command and Tempest. I was never great at these games but had no issue shoving quarters into the box to get my 5 minutes of fun.

Beating a high score was out of the

question. You had to be in your 20's or 30's, have a ton of extra quarters and time to be able to beat high scores. I visited the arcades infrequently. So I never really got a chance to master any of those games. There were guys who I would always see on the same machines and sure enough, they were posting up high scores. There was this sub shop on Massachusetts Avenue called 3 Aces, where you could play the latest tabletop games. I remember going to lunch with a buddy one summer day and watching this guy obliterate the Asteroids high score. We were utterly amazed at his skill. No matter how many asteroids were on the screen, he could clear them out, level after level. We could only dream of having this guy's skills.

My cousin, Perry Mercer, decided one day to become the master of Atari's Star Wars arcade game. It was one of our favorite games back then. He was able to put 50 cents in the machine and play for two hours straight while I dumped five dollars worth of quarters into other games. Every Star Wars machine I came across in Cambridge had his initials, POM, in the number one high score spot. He frequently exchanged high scores with this Japanese woman at the MIT arcade. They'd go back and forth, week after week. I also saw his high score at a corner sub shop in Central Square and at his usual hang out, 1001 Plays on Massachusetts Ave. We would go into that arcade and he would shut it down. There were times where he had to purposely die just so he could put his initials up before they shut the machine off. Those were the days.

Perry and I were always looking for new video game information. We'd subscribe to game magazines like Electronic Games and Video Games & Computer Entertainment. We were nuts for this stuff. Every little bit of information that was available, we had to find. There was nothing like going into an arcade and seeing a new game and wondering where the fuck it came from. The

4

biggest surprise for us was when they brought
Dragon's Lair into 1001 Plays. Perry had gone to
the arcade, saw the game and then called me on
the phone to try and explain what he saw.

> Perry: "You have to see this game! It's Laserdisc!"
> Me: "What!? What's Laserdisc?"
> Perry: "It's on a disc, it's different. It's
> incredible. You have to get this guy through a castle
> and slay a dragon. The deaths are hilarious!"
> Me: "What do the graphics look like?"
> Perry: "It doesn't have graphics! It's a cartoon!"
> Me: "No fucking way! And you can play it?! That's not
> possible! I'm going there tomorrow!"

I wasted no time and hit up the arcade the
next day. It was unbelievable. They had this
Dragon's Lair game in the far left side of the
arcade. Everyone was packed around it, but they
had a second screen on top of the arcade cabinet
so everyone could view the action. The game cost
50 cents to play! That was unheard of back then,
but it was the future so everyone was ponying up
their cash to play. When I first stepped up to
the machine, I was as nervous as a virgin on a
first date. I didn't know what to do. The
controls were unlike those of any traditional
arcade game. You had to move a certain way at a
certain time or you would die. Within 3 minutes
I was dead and had to walk away from the machine.
It was so embarrassing that I couldn't muster up
the courage to go up a second time. I just sat
back with all the rest of the cowards and watched
the valiant heroes waste their money left and
right. When someone got further than anyone had
seen, we stared in silence waiting to see what
happened next. There has NEVER been an arcade
experience like this and there never will be.
Dragon's Lair made a huge impact on all of us.
        We weren't just arcade gamers, we also loved
to play games on console. The arcades were where
we went to see new stuff. The magazines could
only tell us so much. The screenshots looked

good, but didn't measure up to or accurately depict the arcade versions game play and animations. That's what the arcade was for. Personally, while I loved playing at home, it was always disappointing to see that the home versions paled in comparison to the arcade versions. Case in point, Pac-Man for the Atari 2600. The very notion that this game was coming out on home consoles blew my mind. I could now experience at home what I had experienced in the arcade. After playing many other arcade ports like Space Invaders, Asteroids and Missile Command, you'd think that I would have been smart enough to know that Pac-Man wasn't going to look anything like the arcade. I put full blame on Atari for their shady marketing. The very first ad for the Atari 2600 version of the game showed arcade footage. I was too stupid to realize that there was no way the Atari 2600 was pulling those graphics off. I believed everything Atari was feeding me. I was fine with Space Invaders and the others. I knew they weren't the same, but the Pac-Man ads led me to believe they figured something out. They unlocked the true power of the Atari 2600. While I didn't understand why the 2600 couldn't do vector graphics and had large sprites and limited colors, I understood that Atari went beast mode with Pac-Man…at least I thought they did!

My aunt lived in California, the birthplace of all video games. She was closer to the game makers and it made sense for her to get the Pac-Man game for me. She promised to send it for my birthday and as it approached, I would walk home from school hoping to see a brown box on my porch. Back then, it wasn't normal to receive brown boxes in the mail as it is today with Amazon. It's still that same exciting feeling, but back then the suspense of hoping to see that box would nearly kill me. My porch was all brick and you couldn't see the contents on it until you literally walked up the stairs. Every day I would walk up those stairs in slow motion only to find no box. After a week or so, the coveted brown box finally arrived. It was about 12x10x4 and was wrapped in brown paper. I grabbed the box and looked at the return address and smiled from ear to ear. I quickly ran into the house and ripped the box open. There it was, Pac-Man for the Atari 2600. It was a generic yellow box with a beautiful looking Pac-Man painting on it, typical of Atari games back in the day. They had these fabulous pieces of artwork but shitty graphics. I opened the box and quickly flipped through the manual. You didn't really need a manual for Pac-Man but this was part of the whole experience. I wanted to feel it, smell it and see it. Since there was no Internet and the marketing campaign was a lie, I had no idea what the game looked like until I popped the cartridge into my Atari system. The screen was blue, not black. This was the first of many bad signs. When I started the game, there was no Pac-Man melody like in the arcades. It was some wacky smash up of peeks and pokes that made no fucking sense. The background was all blue and the maze was made up of yellow blocks. The blocks weren't hollow, they were solid. The pellets were supposed to be small white squares, but instead they were large rectangles that were the same color as the maze blocks. The ghosts were all one color. It was disgusting and I knew it. I couldn't figure out why it didn't look like the arcade version, but at that point in time I had no choice but to play the game. I had hopes of intermissions and fruits that denoting levels of play. It had none of these features, but I kept playing. This was the only version of Pac-Man available for play at home, so I tried my best to enjoy it. Since there were no intermissions, I would pause the game at the beginning of the third level and hum the Pac-Man intermission music. It was boring and endless and I played until I couldn't take it anymore. Pac-Man was by

far the worst arcade to home port I had ever
played.   Donkey Kong was a close second.   It
wasn't until Ms. Pac-Man was released that Atari
stepped up their game.   It didn't have the
intermissions, but the game play was so much
better than Pac-Man, it got a pass from me.   It
had a better color palette and different mazes.
They did a damn good job and renewed my hope!

        During the time of the Atari 2600 I had
noticed that the Atari 400 and 800 computers were
getting better ports of arcade games.   The 800
version of Pac-Man had all the colors, sounds and
graphics of the arcade version.   Missile Command

was nearly identical to its arcade counterpart and the system had games I'd never seen or played anywhere else. I had to get one. My grandfather was into computers at the time and knew my outdated Timex Sinclair wasn't going to cut it, even with the 16K memory upgrade. He had purchased me an Atari 400. This little gem was a full 8-bit computer. It had 8K of internal RAM and a membrane keyboard. What I really wanted was its big brother, the Atari 800. The 800 had an expansion slot and you could upgrade it to 48K of RAM. When I eventually got my Atari 800, my aunt had also picked up a 5 1/4" floppy disk drive. I think at the time it was $150. The games at the time were considered 'next gen' by industry standards. They were very close to the arcade version in both graphics and sound. My cousin Perry also had an Atari 800. One of my high school buddies hooked me up with a shit load of free games. I would always make copies for Perry. We had Kangaroo, Missile Command, Asteroids and a bunch of other stuff I can't even remember. Perry was taking programming at the time and decided to make his own game on the Atari 800. I forget the name of the game, but it involved crossing a desert of randomly generated mines. I was very impressed with his work and had an interest in learning the missile graphics programming system on the Atari 800. Despite reading programming books, my comprehension was sub par at best. I had a wealth of ideas but coding wasn't my thing.

Nothing Can Stop A Gamer

At some point before the NES(Nintendo
Entertainment System) came out, Perry and I were
huge Colecovision heads. We both saved our money
and bought Colecovision systems. Because Perry
was older and actually had a job, he was able to
buy more games. On the other hand, I either had
to save my allowance or plead with my mother or
wait until Xmas or birthdays. I remember begging
my mother for an entire fucking day to buy Ms.
Pac-Man for the Atari 2600 for me. I had to have
it and asked for an entire day, from like 8am -
6pm and she finally caved and bought it. It was
10 times better than Pac-Man and I played until I
fell asleep with the controller in my hand. So
yeah, Perry was able to spend his whole check on
steak and cheese subs and video games because he
was still going to school and living at home.
He'd buy new shit, call me up and tell me about
it and then I'd either take the bus or hop on my
bike for the 4 mile trip to his house in
Cambridge. Hopping on my Huffy 12-speed to go
play new games that I couldn't afford was the
life! Playing at Perry's house was like a
testing ground for me. If he bought something
and I really liked it, I would start saving and
buy it myself. The best part of owning a
Colecovision was the fact that the games were
about 75% arcade perfect! Some of them were even

closer to the arcades like Lady Bug and Mouse Trap.

The Colecovision had a great run. It was shortly after the Adam was released that Colecovision just died. This was truly our first heartfelt video game loss. Without new Colecovision games, we had to spend more money in the arcades to get our fix. We still played the games we owned, but there was nothing new on the horizon, at least we thought. I mean, yeah, Atari came out with the 5200, but that was just an Atari 800 in sheep's clothing. Atari wasn't fooling me and Perry. We already had that system and it came with a keyboard, 5 1/4" floppy drive and 64K ram pack! On top of that, we were getting most of our games for free! The arcades, specifically 1001 Plays, became our second home. If we weren't at the arcades or at home playing video games, we were hanging out at one of the numerous comic book stores in Cambridge.

The video game crash sucked! I remember walking into retail outlets in the hopes that some new game was released without our knowledge. There was nothing to be found. We still had our video game magazines which gave us great insight to what was going on. I can't remember reading about the NES or Sega Master System at all. One day video game ads just appeared on TV and the industry was reborn. The thing that was cool about the NES commercials was that they were showing games we were playing in the arcade like Duck Hunt. Yes, I played that in the arcade along with Excitebike on the VS arcade system.

My friend Bubba got the NES shortly after it was released. Perry also procured one for himself. I had had my eyes on the Sega Master System. I had plenty of places to play NES games, so why not try something different? Bubba's father was always on the NES. Every time I went out to his house in Bedford to stay the weekend, his dad was playing Mario Golf. His dad was a golfer and now he was a gamer too! When I finally sat down to play it, I really couldn't understand the system. I mean, what in the fuck was the purpose of the robot? What did it do? Did I really need this slow ass robot to enhance my game play when I could press the buttons much faster myself? What was this Nintendo company thinking!

Perry called me over to check out his Nintendo Entertainment System. He had Ice Climber, Duck Hunt and I think every other game that launched with the system. We went nuts! Perry was very anal retentive about packaging his games. The NES games had a cardboard box, a clear plastic bag covering the cartridge and another plastic cover protecting the contacts on the cartridge. EVERY TIME WE PLAYED A GAME HE PUT EVERYTHING BACK THE WAY IT CAME! I was like, "Perry, why in the hell do you save the plastic wrap and the cardboard box?!" He would always say, "Because I take care of my shit!" Unbeknownst to us, Perry was becoming a game collector who today has a collection worth an easy 6 figures! He actually has a mint condition copy of Tengen's Tetris game. Tetris at one point was an arcade game released by Atari. Tengen was Atari's NES game company. Tengen released the only true arcade version of Tetris. Because Nintendo had a license to release a Tetris console game, they had Tengen pull their games off the shelves. I repeat, Perry has a mint condition version of this game. An 85+ version of this game sells for $800.

Living in the east coast means dealing with 4 seasons. The worst season for gaming was winter. Winter meant we had to brave snow storms to get to retail outlets like Childworld or Toys R Us just to buy games. There are times Perry and I would wait for a bus in the snow for an hour just to get to Toys R Us and see if anything new came out. Sometimes we knew stuff was in stock because we had called ahead, but back then there was no game release Tuesday. We also

didn't have the Internet, so new stuff could drop
without our knowledge. Imagine the looks on our
faces when we show up to Toys R Us and there's a
new game on the shelf that we've never heard of
before. This meant we had to pick up the box,
look at the pics on the back of the box and read
the descriptions just to determine if it was
worth buying. This was the case with Megaman,
which we purchased at Software Etc. We looked at
that cover and were like, "WTF!"? It was a man
in armor but to me it looked like a robot. It was
published by Capcom and that was good enough for
the both of us, so Perry bought it. Megaman
ended up being not only one of our most grueling
gaming experiences, but also our favorite. We
would both take turns playing and work our way
through each level. The music, game play,
complexity of bosses and variety of levels were
all top notch.

Beating a game back then was very
satisfying. At the time we didn't have the
luxury of reference tools such as YouTube or
Twitch, but rather used our own skills and
experiences. Megaman was top tier and we killed
it along with many other games too. Capcom had
some of the best games back then. We played
through Megaman, Ghosts and Goblins and Trojan.
Then we hit our Konami period with Castlevania,
Rush'n Attack and Contra. I remember when Perry
picked up Wizards and Warriors. By this time I
had bought my mother an NES so she could play
Galaga and 1 or 2 other games she loved. So
Perry brought it to my house for a first run
through. The game was super hard. In fact,
Wizards and Warriors was the Dark Souls of that
generation. We played all day long and made it
to the final level. By the time we reached the
final level, we were getting hammered left and
right by the boss, but we were close to having
his pattern figured out. It was late and we were
foolishly playing on the living room television.
My dad was in his room for a couple of hours so

we had full reign of the TV. Just when we were getting close to beating the game, he came into the living room and told us we had been playing long enough and to turn it off so he could watch TV. We pleaded with him about the fact that we were on the final boss, but he didn't understand any of that shit. We shut the game off and Perry went home. Let me remind you, there were no game saves back then and we had spent at least 5-6 hours getting to the end. Perry went home that night and started all over again and beat the game by 2:30 that morning.

When I picked up my SMS (Sega Master System), it was a brave new world. The games were different and had more color than the games on NES. Perry was now coming over my house to play Alex Kidd In Wonderland, Black Belt and Rocky. Perry LOVED the SMS as much as I loved the NES. We would both complement each other because I had what he didn't have and vice versa. We were complete gamers! I remember Perry playing Rocky and saying, "How come they don't have games like this on NES!"? I always thought that NES had the better games, but their arcade ports weren't like the arcades. For instance, Double Dragon felt like an entirely different game on NES than at the arcade. The SMS version of Double Dragon was an arcade port. It had weaker graphics but played and followed the arcade game as it should. Ninja Gaiden NES was a much worse culprit as it had absolutely nothing whatsoever to do with the arcade game! The SMS also had two slots for games. One was a regular cartridge slot and the other was a card slot for games requiring less memory.

Looking back on how Perry and I loved the games we didn't own reminds me of how ignorant gamers are today. I truly don't understand the fanboy culture. When we were coming up we did everything possible to play games we didn't have access to. There was a camraderie and respect among gamers. Instead of bashing each others consoles and games, we questioned what was better, Sonic or Mario? The first time I actually started hating on a company was when Nintendo used their shitty business practices to prevent releases of competitor's games. Tengen's Tetris fell off the face of the earth and Sunsoft's Batman for Sega Genesis didn't release in the states until almost a year after its Japanese release. This didn't stop me from continuing to support Nintendo for many years. Perry and I were the essence of what a true gamer should be. We played everything and anything across a variety of platforms we could get our hands on. Our snowy treks on foot and by bus could take us upwards of 3+ hours but to us it was well worth it. When Perry finally got a car, it was a wrap! We would drive all over the city in search of games. If it was out of stock in one store, we would simply go to the next, hell-bent on finding the latest and greatest game. We were constantly checking out retail ads and outlets to see when new games came out. You really had to put in leg work back then to find new games. Gamers have it easy today and take it for granted. If we only had to wait until Tuesday to get new titles, the hunt would have been much easier.

Summer In Silicone Valley

It all started back in the 80's. I used to spend the summer in California while my cousin, Perry Mercer, gamed the summer away in Boston. We've always been huge gamers. We were so geeky that we would write video game reviews on paper and mail them to each other during these summers. I can remember a specific review he sent me of Roc N' Rope for the Colecovision. He actually hand wrote the review. I was amazed and motivated to do the same. I started writing reviews of games I played while in California. I would write on an IBM PC Clone using Wordstar 2000. My aunt was setup with all that and a printer too! We did this back and forth a few times during the summer. The cool thing about being close to Silicone Valley was seeing all the game companies. While on the highway, we drove past the Data East offices and I freaked out! I got to play tons of new shit at the local Chuck E. Cheese before my cousin could in Boston. Cali was the place to be if you were a gamer. Being 46 years old now, I was exposed to a lot of classic games in the arcades before they were on consoles. California was the stomping ground for new arcade games because that's where Japan was sending all their new shit. If I wasn't gaming at Chuck E. Cheese, I was at Great America's huge arcade. If not there, it was an arcade at the local mall. I always found an arcade and in it I found new games. I would write about my experiences and mail it to Perry. We were really dedicated, but we weren't Arnie Katz and Bill Kunkel, who were the gods that gave us Electronic Games magazine. We could only hope to be like them one day. I had no idea what it took to write a video game magazine and at that point in time I didn't care. I just had to play everything!

Summers at my aunt's house introduced me to PC gaming. I had already gamed on Apple II computers before, but PC gaming was something new. She had a beast PC clone with a 20MB hard drive! I lost my mind! There was no Windows at the time, but she had this cool DOS-based interface that allowed you to see all your files and launch your apps and games. I became addicted to connecting to BBS(Bulletin Board System). BBS ran off of single computers and basically allowed you to access the files on those computers remotely. You could also have forum discussions and chats and play text based games. I did all that shit and more! I used to download shareware to my aunt's computer and then play it. I was exposed to clones of arcade games, adult games, homebrew and addicting text based games.

I was so hooked on BBS technology, that one day I built my own PC and turned it into a WWIV BBS. I loaded it up with games and pornographic images. I read through all the software setup documentation and had a perfectly operating BBS. I listed it in ComputorEdge magazine. ComputorEdge was a free, locally printed magazine that had a list of BBS sites on a dedicated page every week. Once it got out there I would watch my modem take a call, connect a user, download porn and disconnect. Mind you, these were only images, not videos. I had a 56K modem running the site and also connected a dot matrix printer to print connection logs. I would come home from

work and it was the same thing, over and over
again. Someone would connect, download porn and
disconnect. No one was playing games or chatting
in the forums or anything. After a short time
running it, I finally shut it down.

After many summer trips to California, I
finally decided to move there after graduating
high school. I stayed with my aunt and truly
loved the experience. The plan was to work for a
year, get my residency and then go to school. I
originally went to Southwestern College to become
an engineer. After 2 semesters of CAD/CAM
engineering classes I discovered that it wasn't
for me. I then switched to Computer Science and
was bored cuz I could have taught the class. The
creative arts was where my heart was so I took
multi-track recording and photography. I learned
multi-track recording and the basics of film
photography. Many years later I went back to
Southwestern and took several film classes and
learned how to edit video. I really wish I
started off in the creative arts, but sometimes
you just don't know what you want in life. It
was these creative arts that got me into radio
and podcasting and also journalism. It was this
plus my love of video games that started
everything. My love of video games would one day
key me into the business side of video game
journalism, which I had to learn to be
successful.

The Consumer Electronics Show

When I first decided to create a video game magazine, I knew that the CES(Consumer Electronics Show) would be a great way to make some industry contacts. My first big convention was Comdex. Comdex was a computer oriented convention that was held at the LVCC(Las Vegas Convention Center). Every single company that created software or hardware components for computers attended Comdex. At the time, it was the biggest computer convention in the world. Comdex was later usurped by the CES which has been running since 1967. CES had shows in Chicago and Vegas twice a year.

My first real exposure to CES was in Las Vegas. I drove to Vegas from San Diego with my friend Jason. He had gone to see all the cool show cars and new automotive tech. The cars at this show were amazing! They were super clean and had sound systems loud enough to be heard across a small city. It was cool, but wasn't too exciting for me. I liked being there because of the environment. Big conventions can easily pull you away from your monotonous life and temporarily transport you to a fantasy world with future tech and booth babes. My journey's purpose became clear when I stumbled upon the South Hall of the LVCC. The South Hall was entirely composed of video game booths. Sega and Nintendo has the largest booths and smaller third party companies were situated in the extra space around the two behemoths. I was completely blown away. Here I was in Vegas looking at cars all morning and video game nirvana was right there in the South Hall. I told Jason I would meet him later and lost myself in the moment. There were screens with playable video games everywhere I looked. I couldn't turn my head without seeing an unreleased video game. I was in heaven! I covered the entire South Hall in a few hours and went back every day until we drove back home to San Diego.

When I first got back home, I told Perry about the show. He was super excited about it and wanted to check it out for himself. I had to figure out a way to get both of us to CES so he could witness everything that I did. After waiting one year, Perry was going to fly into San Diego for his first CES. Jason and my friend Steve from work would accompany Perry and I on a 4 hour road trip to the show in Vegas. Unfortunately on the way to San Diego, Perry's flight got stuck in Pittsburgh due to a snowstorm. The snowstorm delayed the flight out of Boston, but he was promised that the flight out of Pittsburgh would wait for his flight to land before leaving. When he arrived, his flight had already taken off and there wasn't another flight til the next day. This was day one of the four day CES so due to Perry not showing up until the next day, we were going to miss two days of the show. Even though Perry was offered free hotel and dinner, he was furious! If you think about it, I had prepped him for this show a year earlier and his anticipation was beyond epic. The airline was screwing this all up for him. In his fury after arguing with the lady at the ticket counter, he slid his duffel bag across the top of the counter knocking down all the brochures. When he told me this story I lost it!

I didn't know my cousin had it in him. I mean,
I've seen him yell at his screen numerous times
and different video games. I thought that anger
was limited to video games, not people
encroaching on his video game fun. Perry arrived
the next night and we drove in late. We fully
enjoyed the last two days of the show and vowed
to somehow make it a yearly pilgrimage.

The next time we would attend the CES was in
Chicago, shortly after we started production of
Video Game Time magazine. Little did we know, it
would be the last CES we went to for gaming.
They dedicated a whole portion of the show to
video games. They did this in an effort to
appease video game publishers who weren't happy
sitting in the South Hall tent at the Las Vegas
CES. It wasn't enough for them as they had
already started making moves to start their own
show and leave the CES for good. Many of the
publishers we talked to kept mentioning this
thing called E3(Electronic Entertainment Expo).
We had no idea what they were talking about, but
we had to figure out what this E3 thing was.
There was no website for E3 at the time so I
eventually dug deep enough and got all the
information about the show from a publisher who
was involved with it. E3 stayed on my radar from
that last trip to CES, all the way up until we
first walked into the Los Angeles Convention
Center in 1995 for the first E3.

I still attend CES today, but not every
year. It seems that lately I've been going every
other year as it's not worth the trip to Vegas to
see a bunch of TV's and cell phones that looked
like the same ones released the previous year. I
do love technology though and it's my reason for
being drawn back to the show, time and time
again. In fact, it's one of the few shows that I
still attend along with any show that's bass
fishing related.

The Rise And Fall of Video Game Time

I had spent some years working for Databased Advisor magazine. While I was there, I learned everything I could about PC's, databases and magazine publishing. My second love is writing and producing Hip-Hop music. I had a sequencer and drum machine at the time and no PC or equipment to produce a magazine. At the time I was trying to figure out how to get a PC, my roommate ran into some money and wanted to pay for recording an album. I couldn't believe he was offering me this opportunity. I think I took at least a day to think about it and I knew it would cost a lot of money and there was a big chance we wouldn't get a deal or even a foot in the door to discuss a deal. Steven had no experience in the industry and neither did I. It would have been really hard for us and I didn't want Steven to waste his money on this. I told him how hard the music industry was to get into and instead convinced him to put his money into publishing a video game magazine. He knew I was a video game super nerd and agreed with the idea. We would print a full color magazine, give it out for free at E3 and sell subscriptions and advertising to pay for future magazine production. I contacted

Perry,and started looking for a staff to help us with the magazine.

The very first staff member I discovered was Matt Jones. Shortly after the Atari Jaguar came out, I went to Software Etc., like I usually did, to see what new games came out. I met one of the clerks and started asking him about the Jaguar and found out that he had purchased one. We chatted for a bit and then I left. The next day I had an epiphany and called back the store to get a hold of him. He wasn't working that day so I left a message for him to call me. I figured that having a Jaguar writer on the staff would be a huge boon! He called me back and accepted my offer to write for Video Game Time magazine. He covered the entire Jaguar section and introduced me to his friend Rob Hill who had recently bought a 3DO. Rob became our 3DO writer. At some point I had to tell Matt to stop calling me his editor, as I was more than that to him and he was more than a staff writer to me. Matt and I have now been friends for 22 years and have had many crazy adventures together, mostly involving video games. Rob later went on to become a game producer.

At the time we started all of this, there was no Internet. I was using Compuserve and Perry was using Prodigy. We scoured the services for writers until Perry discovered Art Lincoln and I found Doug Boehner. Art was only 15 years old but he was a good writer. He wasn't allowed into E3 at the time due to the age limit of 17. I was going to get him into the show anyways. Since he was under 18, I had to talk to his parents before they let him fly out to San Diego to be under my care for a week. They gave him the go ahead and before we knew it, we were driving up to LA for E3. I don't know how we managed to do it, but I snuck this 15 year old into E3 and we didn't get caught.

Art Lincoln posing with Ho Sung Pak(Liu Kang) at the first E3

Doug had gone to the last CES with us before
E3 was a thing. I can't remember where he was
from, but he was a constant source of laughter
for me and Perry. To get from our hotel to the
Chicago CES, we had to grab a shuttle. It was a
long ride in the rain and wind. We got all the
way to the convention center and waited in line
to get our passes. Doug had left his ID back at
the hotel. I looked at him and asked him, "How
in the fuck could you forget the most important
item you need to get into this show?". He had no
clue how he forgot it, so I told him I would see
him when he got back to the convention center.
These trips were always expensive, but Perry and
I always booked rooms. Doug crashed in our room
with us on the floor. Perry told him to get some
support for his back, but Doug said he would be
fine. He woke up the next day moaning, "My
baaaack! Oh my baaack!". Of course Perry and I
died laughing because he didn't listen to us the
previous night. I think I originally connected
with Doug because he had purchased a Japanese
Sega Saturn and would be a great asset to the

magazine. Doug didn't do much after E3 and we never heard of him again.

Having put together a staff, I needed content. I started grabbing all of my video game boxes and manuals to find phone numbers. I called each and every video game publisher I could and asked for their fax number. I created a logo and letterhead in Microsoft Word and entered all of the phone numbers and names I had into Winfax Pro. I had over 50 faxes to send out. My intro letter had a mission statement and details about what Video Game Time was going to be. I started sending out faxes and went to sleep. Once the faxes were done, I started calling people and making more contacts. I needed anything and everything I could get to publish my first issue.

The first true contact I ever made was Jay Malpas from Data East. This guy was too cool for school. He was the first publisher support I ever had. He sent me ROMS for games that weren't even finished so that I could write previews. Back in those days cartridges were still popular because of the Super NES and Sega Genesis. So if you wanted to preview anything for the system, you were sent a cartridge. These cartridges had no stickers or fancy plastic, just the circuit board and chips. After you were done previewing the game, you had to mail the cartridge back. I was so grateful with Jay and Data East that I gave them a free ad on the back page of the magazine. I did the same for Readysoft on the inside.

Through my hard work I had gained support from Data East, Readysoft, Sega, The 3DO Company, Atari, Nintendo, Crystal Dynamics, Sunsoft, Universal, Shiny Entertainment, Capcom, American Laser Games and JVC. Games, images, press releases and systems were arriving at my front door. I was having Perry and our small group of writers send their reviews through Compuserve and regular mail.

After many sleepless nights, I had laid out our first issue of Video Game Time. I worked long

and hard and submitted everything to the printer.
Aside from them screwing up the quote and my
roommate having to pay more than we wanted, we
had a beautiful, fully colored video game
magazine. Now we needed to distribute it.

I sent copies to all the companies that
supported us. The free ads I had placed in the
magazine added that professional touch. At this
point they were taking us seriously. I had 3,000

copies of the first issue printed. They were in
boxes stacked in my garage. I had distributed a
couple hundred at local Electronic Boutique shops
but needed to take the rest to LA for the very
first E3(Electronic Entertainment Expo). If
you've ever been to an E3 before, you know that
they have these bins for free magazine give
aways. We would stack about 100 magazines inside
the bin, go check out the show floor and come
back to find empty bins. People were grabbing the
magazine. How cool was that? This was guerrilla
magazine distribution at its best! My only
concern at this point was if they were going to
subscribe or not.

When we first walked into E3 we were
completely overwhelmed. Here was a show strictly
about video games that had the scale of the CES.
Yes, it was much smaller than the CES, but still
HUGE. The LA Convention Center was broken up
into two main halls; North and South. All the
majors had gigantic booths and they were
surrounded by smaller booths. So Sega, Sony and
Nintendo had the biggest footprints with EA's
being slightly smaller. Every other third party
publisher or hardware manufacturer had about one
quarter of the space. You literally had to pick
one hall and spend a day there or go back and
forth like I did. To make things easier, I
assigned publishers to all of our staff to cover.
After they covered their publisher, they could go
and check out whatever they wanted. Our team
consisted of Perry, Matt Jones, Doug Boehner, Art
Lincoln, Steven Campbell and myself.

From left to right; Steven Campbell, Torrence Davis, Matt Jones, Perry Mercer, Rob Hill and Doug Boehner

The very first E3 marked the beginning of the new video game era. Sega had just dropped the Sega Saturn for $399. I had already received mine in the mail and was given the complete library of launch games at E3. I met a lot of my contacts face to face and established great relationships. We were invited to parties and previews and treated like kings. All the major publishers had parties after the shows on certain days. We tried to get in as many as we could. Usually during the 4 days we always had a meal ticket somewhere in town. Sega and Sony would battle back and forth trying to one up each other with the biggest and best parties. Sometimes Sega had the best parties and sometimes it was Sony. Sega had this bomb party in LA where they had Filter and another year they had Brian Setzer at the House of Blues. I think the best party ever was the Sony party at E3 '98 in Atlanta. This party was super hard to get into, but because I knew people I was able to get all 5 of my staff access. Sony rented out an entire parking garage. They had

the Foo Fighters doing a whole concert, offered
up free booze and cigars and food up the wazoo!
I was eating skewered shrimps and every other
hors d'oeuvres that flew past me. I had never
been drunk up until this point in my life. I was
28 years old at the time and my best friend Bubba
told me he could drink me under the table. I had
beers, rum and coke, screw drivers and straight
Vodka. I was fine and he was dumping his drinks
on the floor when I wasn't looking. At some
point in time the alcohol kicked in and I became
an emotional wreck. I couldn't believe they let
me get drunk and didn't tell me to not mix my
alcohol. Bubba was way past gone before he
started dumping drinks. We were a mess. The
party ended and we were supposed to pick up a
Sony hat on the way out. I remember getting up
and then I was at the top of the stairs. I
literally blacked out and have no recollection of
getting that hat, but I got it. I guess I was so
plastered that I saw some PR ladies from Virgin
Games and I started ranting at them for not
sending us review copies. I was a complete mess.
When we got back to the hotel, I was unable to
get undressed to go to bed. Perry helped me get
my shoes off and then I headed to the bathroom to
throw up. I kneeled down in front of the toilet
but couldn't yak to save my life. Perry slapped
my back as hard as he could and I spit out my
insides like Linda Blair did in the Exorcist. I
thought I was safe and went to sleep.

The next day was going to be HUGE! My 20th
Century Fox Games contact, Chris Kingrey, was
going to introduce me to Gillian Anderson before
she signed autographs. I was going to have an up
close and personal meeting with her. I woke up
that morning to dry heaves and dehydration. It
made no sense to me. Why was I still drunk, but
with a headache and an extreme thirst for water?
I drank a glass of water and then my stomach
pushed all the way into my spine. I'm getting
nauseous just writing about this. Anyways, I

pushed on, showered, got dressed and headed to E3
for meetings and Gillian Anderson. Bubba had
thrown up all over the floor and stayed at the
hotel. When I got to the convention center, I
couldn't really move well and had no energy to do
anything. I went to the press room to lay down
on this beautiful black leather couch. I figured
I would miss out on early appointments and rest
until it was time to meet Gillian Anderson. I
laid on the couch for about 2 hours and then got
up to head to the show floor. I got nauseous and
headed to a stall in the mens room. Once again my
stomach pushed all the way into my spine. I was
standing up this time so it probably looked like
an alien was trying to burst out of my back. I
couldn't understand why this was still going on.
It was like I had the stomach flu but it was
induced by alcohol. I dry heaved a spoonful of
bile, washed up and hit the show floor. When I
got to the floor I moved slowly to 20th Century
Fox's booth. I saw Chris and he waved me over to
take me to meet Gillian. I started walking over
to him and he came back and stopped me. He said
they were ready for her to sign autographs so
there was no time for me to meet her. I was so
bummed out. If I hadn't been drunk and was on
the show floor earlier I could have met her. It
was a lesson learned.

I slowly pushed through the day walking like
a zombie from booth to booth. Whenever I got to
a booth I would perk up and compose myself
professionally. I met with several of my
contacts and got the job done. I would drink a
little water here and there, hoping I wouldn't
yak all over the show floor. One booth had free
popcorn and I hadn't had anything to eat all day.
I grabbed the bag and ate like one popcorn kernel
every 20 minutes. By the time the show was over,
my appetite was back and we hit up a diner. It
took me about 10 years before I could drink rum
and Coke again. Every time I thought about it or
smelled it, I would get nauseous.

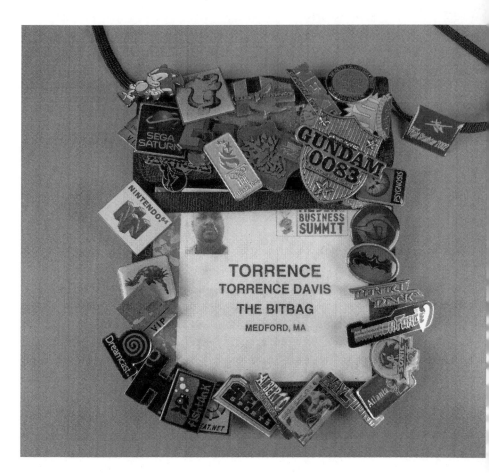

The first years of E3 were the best. Not
many can forget the impact Playstation made in
1995 when people first got a chance to play on
the PS1. It was amazing! There were so many
games and so many people. We were extremely
overwhelmed but we loved every minute of it.
Sony and Sega offered alcoholic beverages and
sandwiches in special press areas in their
booths. Sony's booth had two levels and required
a special VIP pin to get to the second floor.
They had a bar and sandwiches too! I was able to
get pins every year. E3 was our new Christmas
and waiting a year for it made me feel like a kid
again. In the early days of E3 we used to make a

31

Last minute sweep on Day 3 to get all the stuff
publishers didn't want to take home. I remember
getting all kinds of stuff from Nyko and Nuby.
They were the hottest accessory manufacturers
back then and they loved us. We also got X-Band
units to take home with us. We always had huge
bags of press releases and all kinds of gaming
goods. It's not like that anymore though.
You're lucky to walk out of E3 with a sticker
these days.

I'll never forget that first E3 for as long
as I live. I've tried to explain to many people
how incredible it was and there are really no
words. It was like gaming nirvana. That first
show was a grand slam and I learned so much. I
had left the show with new relationships formed,
a stack of business cards, press kits and enough
info to get started on my second issue. I started
to wonder how I was going to fund my next issue.
We didn't have the money and subscriptions
weren't coming in. The problem with giving away
free magazines is that readers expect the next
issue to be free too. I had no way of putting out
another issue. I even contacted the same printers
that were printing Diehard Gamefan magazine and
got a great price, but just didn't have the
money.

I was introduced to the World Wide Web in
its early stages and thought it was a waste of
time. When I was trying to decide what to do
about VGT, I did some research on the Internet. I
had an epiphany and decided to create vgt.com.
Everything I knew about magazine publishing was
now useless as I was entering a new era, so I had
to learn publishing on the web. After learning
some HTML I started creating the website.

I worked as hard on the website as I did the
magazine. I remember it having a start page and a
counter. That was real popular back then. It was
very basic looking and had no flair. It was,
however, vgt.com. After some time and some more
research, I learned about image maps and tables.

I redesigned the site and it had flair, great colors and lots of links. We had news, game reviews, cheats, movie reviews and kung fu movie clips and reviews. Our cheats and movie reviews, especially Kung Fu Theatre, were very popular.

There weren't many gaming websites when we launched. Well, there weren't that many professional ones. The fact that we had a dot com meant something to game publishers. There were tons of Little Johnnie's Sega Saturn Land websites sitting on Geocities shared space. Of the professional ones I can remember that sprung up and had an impact were gaming-age.com and egm.com. That was pretty much it. Back in the late 90's, there were no Alexa ratings, search engine optimization or this thing called CPM(Cost Per Thousand). There was no way to track how well a site was doing. The best you could do was get high on the yahoo.com search engine.

I probably could have secured advertising for the site, but never cared about making money off of it. We were getting so much stuff in the mail, it seemed criminal to sell ad space. We were saving thousands a year on video game purchases. Anytime I needed something I could get it. One of the controller ports on my PS1 broke. I emailed Sony and had a new PS1 in the mail the next day. I tried hard to get one of the blue debugging units, but there was a huge line for those. We played beta versions of games using one of the old tricks to play imports on the PS1. In fact, I still have a PS1 game that never made it to market.

Not only were we getting shit loads of games to review, we were also getting A-class treatment in other areas. You hear this talk about how publishers shower editors with gifts and other goodies in hopes of getting good reviews? Well, we got to experience that a lot. We would get limo rides from E3 to free dinners every year with Home Media. Sega always had the best parties and we were always invited. The biggest Sony

party ever was in Atlanta, GA during E3. We got
in because of people we knew at Sony that made
special accommodations for us.

The biggest goodies came in other forms. One
was a day at the Playboy mansion for the award
ceremony of the Shiny Entertainment Wild 99
gaming marathon. We met playmates new and old, I
got to shit on Hugh Heffner's toilet in his
arcade and we consumed all of their free food.
Too bad our digital cameras sucked back then. We
had taken pictures, but lost them when our web
server host went belly up. Another publisher
that loved spending money on the press was
Psygnosis. If you ever wondered why they went out
of business, it's probably because of those spur
of the moment trips they used to plan. They would
call me on a whim and ask to have someone sent
out to preview their games. Perry, the Senior
Editor, got flown out to Coeur D'Alene Golf
Course for two days, all expenses paid. He got to
play 18 holes of golf, stuff his belly with steak
and lobster and wine and got a chance to see
Psygnosis' new golf game. They paid for
everything including a limo ride from the
airport. The second time they called me was to
preview their snowboarding game. No one could
make this trip because of the short notice. In
fact, all the editors at other publications had
trouble making the trip too. Only one editor was
able to go and apparently he got a new snowboard,
gloves, goggles, boots, jacket, a free day at the
slopes and a preview of their game.

We were considered A-list and didn't even
realize it. We were attending events and parties
with the likes of Dave Halverson and Ed Semrad. I
had run into Ed Semrad several times at E3. He
sat behind me on the shuttle back to the hotel
and I asked him why EGM gave Third World War a
bad review. He claimed that they didn't. I guess
he didn't read that issue. He reminded me of Bill
Murray in person.

E3 was always great. It got better every

year, peaked in 2000 and then went downhill. Getting into E3 became more difficult every year. There was so much paperwork needed to qualify credentials, that it became a nauseating task. I went from just sending business cards to sending a large envelope with business cards, signatures, letterheads and a few fingers. Unlike the CES, they never kept a database of who qualified as press the previous years. With the CES you literally pressed a button on their website and you were in.

We still enjoyed E3. I remember seeing Team Fortress 2 in 2000…or 1999. I can't quite remember. It was on the PC and looked totally different. I also remember seeing Duke Nukem Forever and getting really excited about it. We had full access to everything at E3. They would feed us every day in the press room and as technology got better we were able to update the website from the show floor. We had images up pretty fast. Interact had all their new Dreamcast accessories on display in their booth and didn't allow photos. I took some anyways and by the time I got home they were all over the net with credit to vgt.com.

I ran the site well into the Dreamcast era. Playstation 1 was still huge, Dreamcast made a splash and the PS2 had just hit the shelves. We were bored doing reviews. A lot of the games that were coming out either sucked or were "me too" games that offered nothing different than the others we had already reviewed. I hated updating the site. I wasn't aware of dynamic HTML or how to link everything up to a database. Every time we updated the site we had to create a bunch of new HTML files. The E3 updates were huge and required tons of uploads. I grew tired of it and so did everyone else. I did another rehash of the website using flash and the navigation looked great but everything else sucked.

I decided in late 2003 to shut the site down. I didn't know where to go with it and the

technology was moving faster than I could keep
up. There were tons of video game sites popping
up everywhere. Of all the sites that popped up in
the mid 90's, only one of them still stands…
gaming-age.com. They stuck to it and haven't
changed their format at all since their
inception. I wanted to dabble in film and
photography and I did. I had already been taking
some film classes and helped with producing,
editing, sound design and special effects on a
few shorts. I wrote and directed my
first short in 2004.

I actually attended a few E3 conventions
post 2003. They all sucked. I remember one year
it was made impossible to have meetings because
so many people were packing into booths to get
free t-shirts. It was a mess. I saw the launch of
the Xbox and after laughing at it decided to get
one thanks to Wreckless.

In the midst of attending film festivals and
looking for work, I discovered some web
programming languages and the dawn of Web 2.0. I
found ways to dynamically update websites with
the use of MySQL databases. It was the coolest
thing ever for me and I wish I had discovered
this years ago. I was urged by my editors to
create a new vgt.com. I had already sold the
domain so had to start with something new that I
had on my mind for years. After a few weeks of
reading and planning, thebitbag.com was born.

The Bitbag

For many years before the Internet, I always wanted to have a digital magazine about computers and technology. I wanted to call it The Bitbag. I had planned to do it using Microsoft's Help system. With this system, you could make a table of contents and link to the information throughout the document. You could also add imagery to enhance the text based content. It was PERFECT! I never actually did the magazine, but instead did a HipHop magazine called DigIt. This was my first time going through the process and pretty much creating a proof of concept. It worked, but then this thing called the Internet happened.

After the demise of vgt.com, I was content sitting on the sidelines playing World Of Warcraft for hours on end. I helped run one of the biggest guilds on our server. We were doing record times in Molten Core and were selling slots to this raid for in game gold. It got so bad that I can remember both my roommate and I putting in 8+ hours to clear Molten Core and other instances. WoW showed me that PC gaming was more social and fun than console gaming. I bought the Dreamcast, PS2, Gamecube and OG Xbox. After the dust settled, the only console left to play on was PS2. I had played Asheron's Call and beta tested many other MMO games on PC and WoW

was the end all. It wasn't until the Xbox 360
was released that my interest in console gaming
started coming back. All this time my friend
"Candid" Anthony Canepa kept asking me to do
another VGT site. I was so amazed with what they
were doing with the Xbox 360 and PS3, that I
bought both consoles. I picked up a 360 for $360
from Dell in 2006, then later that year bought a
new 80gb PS3 off of Craigslist for $399. Guy who
sold it to me thought it was a 60gb at first, so
I got a great deal! I slowly started playing
less WoW and more console games. I would only
show up for meetings and raids and nothing else.
Consoles had me again and my PC was too weak to
play anything cooler than WoW on it. It was at
this point that Anthony wasn't going to shut up
unless I created a new gaming site. Every time we
got together he would bring up how awesome
VGT.com was and that I should do it again.

Anthony wanted me to make another site but
for all the wrong reasons. When I looked at the
landscape of gaming back then, there were a lot
of idiots consumed by this console war. They
were spouting misinformation and hate because
they didn't like the competing console. Most of
this vitriol was found on N4g.com. Websites were
popping up left and right to either discredit
Xbox 360 or PS3. It didn't help that the media
was bias against Sony at the time. It really
sucked and I thought to myself, "These gamers
need to be educated"! I managed to score a
second shift tech support job for the military.
Late at night there were no calls coming in so I
would surf the net all night long. I scoured the
Internet for ways to produce the website in a
quick fashion. Wordpress was the key to giving
birth to The Bitbag, but I still had a lot to
learn. Most of the blogs coming out at that time
were using Wordpress, Drupal or Joomla. Since
Drupal or Joomla sounded like software that
coders would be happy with, I chose Wordpress.
It had more support, more plugins and an easier

learning curve. Now that I found the software, my goal was to work on the site while working my night shift job. All I had to do was come up with a logo and figure out a color scheme and how to post content. Wordpress was backed by an SQL database. This was something I was already familiar with. What was cool is I could update the site without ever entering a line of HTML! This was Web 2.0! All I could think about is what if I had this tech when VGT.com was up and running?

So thebitbag.com was finally born. I threw it into the sea of hundreds of other gaming sites. Wordpress was my savior and gave me the content management system I wish I had years ago. I could easily add content via an admin panel and it would save it to a database. No more HTML uploads.

Now I needed content. I had lost my contact list and didn't even know who was who in the industry anymore. When I was doing vgt.com, Dave Karraker was at Access PR. At the time I started thebitbag.com, he was still at Sony. My Microsoft contacts had disappeared too. They were a third party company that MS didn't use anymore. I was starting all over again and unlike before, it was going to be much tougher. My goal this time, however, was to do everything right that I had done wrong before. That meant search engine optimization and traffic farming in the hopes of selling ad space.

I first starting going to all the game publisher's websites to get press information. My initial stop was Capcom.com and surprisingly, the same two people that were working there 8 years ago were still there. I let them know who I was and that I had started a new site. They added me to their press list but they now had strict rules in regards to review materials. You had to have an Alexa rating of at least 100,000 to request games to review. "What?!?! What the fuck is Alexa?!" is all that crossed my mind. Thanks to

Google and a few searches, I found alexa.com.
When I first searched on thebitbag.com, we were
ranked 9 million plus. All that came to mind was
that I was never going to get any kind of review
materials if all the game publishers used Alexa.

I continued my search for contacts. I went
the long and hard way to get a Microsoft contact.
They were really cool and gave me all the names
and email addresses I needed. I put together an
intro letter, making sure to note that I used to
run vgt.com in the hopes that someone remembered
me. After my first contact was made, Microsoft
offered full support and sent some games for
review. I continued my search and looked hard and
long for Dave Karraker's information. I could
only find his Sony Europe email address. I dug
deeper for about a week and managed to find his
email address on a press release. I sent the same
letter to him and Sony offered support without
question. I think Dave remembered me from when he
was back at Access PR. Another ace in the hole.
Getting Sony and Microsoft were the hard parts.
Everything else came easy after that.

Every month I was gaining more support from
other publishers. I got Sega, Activision, SNK,
Atari, Midway, Koei and a few others. Capcom
still allowed me access to their press site,
which was good enough for what I needed. I was
grateful that these companies were supporting our
cause. I always made sure to thank them whenever
possible.

I put together a staff of writers, some old
and some new, and started pouring out content.
The deal with the writers was that they get to
keep any games I send them to review. Some day
we'll have advertising and then I'll be able to
actually pay them. For now everyone was on board
and enjoying the benefits of writing reviews and
posting news.

My first agenda was for the writers to not
score their reviews. I hate review scores and
will never use them again. If someone comes to

our site looking for advice on a game, the best thing they can do is read the review. With all the hoopla about review scores lately, I think I made the right decision.

Over the course of the first year, our Alexa ratings climbed to 308,000. We moved several million and continued to climb at a rate of 100,000 per month. All I wanted to do was break 100,000 so I could ask Capcom for every version of Devil May Cry, from Sega Saturn to Playstation 3.

What I've learned about this industry is that every site is giving the same exact information. If you aren't breaking news you aren't making news. If you aren't making news you'll never get the traffic you need to sustain yourself through advertising. I've watched this trend through the entire year. There are sites like Gamespot, IGN and Kotaku that have huge followings. Why would any of their readers come to thebitbag.com to find news that is already on the aforementioned sites? So after researching, reading and scanning several sites, I discovered that the only way to be a mover is to find a niche. I found a few untapped niches to exploit. News and reviews are standard fare for any game site, but you need to have something else. Herein lies the whole problem with starting over from scratch. While vgt.com was popular on a very small scale, there weren't many gamers using the web back then. If I kept vgt.com alive, I could have had the motherload of traffic by now.

After getting the site up, I had to decide on what our editorial direction was going to be. I also had to get on some press lists again to get games, E3 access, etc.. It was easy to get back on Sony and Microsoft's press lists, but other publishers were quite difficult. I was now in a time where I wasn't special, magazines were dying and everyone and their mother had a gaming blog. I had a huge mountain to climb. Like with vgt.com I recruited my cousin and some friends to write articles. The first articles I wrote were contradictory articles to what I was seeing on the net. If someone was posting misinformation, I was there to correct it. It was all a part of my 'gamer education' angle. I also dabbled in posting on N4G to capitalize on the vitriol that was being spread on that site. Again, I was posting articles to educate people, but at the same time pissing off a lot of people. It was really easy to pick on Sony at the time because they launched a console for $600 that was difficult for developers to work with. Since N4g was a haven for fanboyism, I sparked many flames. N4g's mods were horrible and part of the problem. There were some that were cool, but for the most part, they capitalized on all the fanboyism and it actually turned into money for them.

N4G eventually became one of my most hated sites. I came to realize that their success was based on everyone else's hard work. They wouldn't be where they were without bloggers on the Internet posting their content in an effort to get more readership. N4G never created any content of their own and made a fuckton of money aggregating others work. It was at this point I decided that I wasn't going to be posting any of my content on the site anymore. At the same time I realized that a lot of our readership came from N4G and I was potentially throwing away a good means of producing traffic. Kotaku, IGN and Gamespot, the biggest sites on the net, made matters worse by posting their content on N4G. I couldn't understand why. These sites were getting 2-4 million hits a day without N4G. I guess there's never a reason to stop growing and they saw N4G as another outlet to grow.

Hard work pays off. There were times when articles were posted on our site that blew up. I couldn't figure out how or why. There was no real formula to it. There are people who will tell you how important SEO(Search Engine Optimization) is and how without good SEO you

42

won't get good Google rank or traffic. There are
people getting paid to setup SEO for websites. I
just used a plugin and our stuff was coming up in
all kinds of Google searches. Sometimes it was
number 1 and because of that, we would get a huge
spike in traffic. We were proving that we didn't
really need N4G…then it happened. Someone sent
me a link to an N4G post that came from IGN, but
the original story was ours. It was Nate Ahern
from IGN who stole a quote that I got from Aaron
Greenberg at Microsoft. He posted the quote,
editorialized it and never credited The Bitbag or
linked back to our site. I released the hounds!
Tons of my fans started tweeting Nate and posting
on IGN's site that they stole my quote. Long
time fan, friend and co-blogger, Jorge Murphy,
was the one who saw the thievery and contacted
me. He also pointed out that Morgan Webb from X-
Play had mentioned our story on her show and
properly quoted us and credited our site. After
getting bombarded by angry tweets from our fans,
Nate finally updated the article on IGN and
linked back to us. He also sent me an email
apologizing:

Hi Torrence,

I'd like to give you my sincerest apologies for
copying that quote from your story on TheBitBag. I
assure you that I do not take something like this
lightly and it was an unintentional oversight on my
part. The article on IGN has been fixed with a proper
callout to your article.

Again, I'm sorry for the screw up.

Sincerely,

Nate Ahearn

And my response:

Thank you so much sir. Even though I can't stand
IGN.com, I have much respect for you for addressing
the issue and fixing.

Thanks again!

Torrence

The Bitbag was a great site! I watched it
grow and transform over the years. I ran it from
2008 - 2012 and decided to close up shop and sell
the site shortly after I lost my job and was
looking to get out of the industry and into
something else. The industry was growing out of
control. There were thousands of blogs all
posting content on N4G and fighting for
attention. Unlike the vgt.com days, there was
actually money to be made on the web now. We
made a few dollars here and there and I was able
to help my staff with some things like food and
hotel but that's it! There was no career to be
made. Money makes money and I had nothing to
start with. I was sick of how the press was not
only viewed by publishers, but how publishers
were treating us as unpaid interns to help market
their products. It got old very fast. I had
done it all and was ready to call it quits. That
and the fact that I didn't feel right making my
staff work so hard when I couldn't pay them. On
top of that, people that I hired to write
articles, rested on their laurels to do podcasts
instead of writing. Now they were doing the
podcasts weekly and I was fine with that, but
they were no longer writing articles. I guess
it's easier to sit there and talk about a subject
or flap your gums for 2hrs than it is to take the
time to write a decent article. This really got
on my nerves. It all just kept piling up and
took the passion out of me. Losing my job was a
blessing in disguise but at the same time, it was
part of the catalyst that made me sell thebitbag
so I could move on to other things. I sold the

site for a mere $2000 and headed into the sunset.
I did however, decide to continue doing the Video
Game Warzone podcast as it was one of my true
loves of creativity.

STFUandPlay

Candid Anthony was always on my case to create new gaming websites. He was the one that talked me into doing The Bitbag. While I was running The Bitbag, he tried his hand at creating a blog and registered the name, STFUandPlay.com. It was an awesome name and he used a smiley face with duct tape across the mouth as a part of his logo. This was his answer to fanboyism. Why waste time fighting about what console is better when you can just be enjoying yourself playing the games? That's what Shut The Fuck Up And Play meant. Anthony always had great ideas, but didn't want to do any of the work. I remember giving him this high speed network card to review. I think it took him like 6 months to review it. I mean, how hard is it to review a NIC(Network Interface Card)? Anyways, at some point Anthony gave up on his blog and wanted me to have the domain to create a new gaming site. I had recently sold thebitbag.com and was pretty much done with it, but the name was so awesome I had to do something with it. He transferred the domain over to me and I started thinking about what I needed to do. I understood the industry. I knew how to create content and enable people, I just needed an idea. I had two ideas I wanted to put into action and one of them could have been met with huge success had it worked out.

My first plan was to get editors from all the sites we knew to contribute content to stfuandplay.com. I contacted people from thekoalition.com, analoghype.com, gamesonsmash.com, Hiphopgamer and a few others. I also brought in some new blood by hiring Tony Polanco. Tony had been a fan of my work for some time and I didn't even know it, but he started his own blog. He said it was just for fun but was interested in writing for me. Jon Shaw had been working with me since the Bitbag days and agreed that it was a great idea. He came along with a few others and we started to communicate. A huge issue in the industry at the time was that IGN, Kotaku, Gamespot and Giant Bomb were getting the bulk of traffic. They were white owned, white run and extremely popular with gamers. Back then you were measured by how much traffic you got. The more traffic you got, the higher your Alexa rankings would be. High Alexa rankings meant that publishers were more likely to support you with review copies, interviews, press junkets and behind closed door access at E3. The way I looked at it is this, if Games On Smash was getting 40,000 hits a month, Analog Hype was getting 25,000, I was able to net about 120,000, Hiphopgamer was getting 230,000 and The Koalition was getting about 120,000, that was a total of 620,000 hits a month collectively. Individually we weren't going to meet much success, but together we would blow up! All of us working together on one site meant that their fans were getting access to my content and my fans were getting access to their content. We would not only bring our talent together, but we'd also bring all of our fans to one spot. The increase in traffic would mean more press goodies for us and more importantly, ADVERTISING! Advertising meant money! If we could bring in money, we could all get paid, pay for hotel, food and flight to E3, etc.

It was a solid plan and a few people were on

board with it, but the majority weren't
interested. I made it clear that I did not
expect them to dump their current sites, but to
produce one or two creative works on
stfuandplay.com, see how it works and then later
make a 100% move. If it didn't work out, they
still had their old site to go back to. If I
could sell my site and do something that would
make our lives better, why couldn't they? One of
the reasons for the disinterest that I kept
hearing from a few people is that they didn't
want me to run the site or be the 'leader'. I
told them that the only thing I wanted from them
was standards in posting. Just follow a set
standard and you can pretty much post what you
want. The problem with black people in business
is that we don't want to work together. It's
that whole "Too many chiefs, not enough Indians"
thing. Everyone wanted to be a chief and no one
was willing to be a warrior as long as I was the
chief. They didn't see the big picture. I even
asked them, "You're putting out one podcast every
few weeks, why not put it amongst a bunch of
other creative works and grow your fanbase"? I
knew it would work but I didn't get enough people
that agreed. I went on to make stfuandplay.com
with the staffers that I hired directly and
everyone else went back to their sites.
Gamesonsmash is now gone and they just recently
started a new site called 1stPlayers.
Analoghype.com is surprisingly still up and
running with a few podcasts here and there.
Hiphopgamer continues his grind and The Koalition
is still steadily producing content and getting
good traffic.

The thing that pisses me of to this day
about this whole plan falling apart is that
shortly after stfuandplay.com launched, a bunch
of editors from a bunch of websites all came
together and created a site called Polygon.com.
They all brought their fanbases with them and
created new content. The site blew up instantly

and is still running today. It is probably one
of the most successful start up gaming sites in
the history of gaming sites. THIS is what I
wanted to do with stfuandplay.com but heads will
be hard.

My second plan for stfuandplay.com was to
disregard the relationship between press and
publisher so we could write what the fuck we
wanted to. I also wanted to release leaked
information about games. This would put us on
the map and at the same time destroy
relationships with publishers. I wanted to prove
to the world that as the press, we don't need
publishers, they need us. Without us, they had
to find other ways to hype their games. They had
to hire REAL interns to post their boring press
releases. I posted so many press releases I
really felt like an unpaid intern at one point.
It was boring and horrible. That had to stop. I
also did away with review scores. If you want
someone to read your reviews, kill the review
scores. We were forward thinking. We started
implementing a lot of plan B and it was working.
The leaks I was given couldn't be published
without the sources permission. I leaked a few
great things, but a lot of it had to be kept
under wraps until right when it was official
during E3. Posting leaks this way was done to
protect my sources. I didn't want anyone to lose
a job for giving me info. So I really never
pissed any publishers off. We went back to
getting free games and doing the same shit we did
for years, but it was great! I had the best
staff I ever had.

I was planning to do a huge site overhaul.
I had learned some web design, but wasn't the
greatest at putting it together. I wasn't a code
head and was forced to learn CSS(Cascading Style
Sheet) just to get STFUandPlay up and running. I
also dumped Wordpress for a platform called
Expression Engine. It was 10 times better than
Wordpress but it meant I had to learn a whole new

package. I spent many nights literally on the brink of tears because I had bugs in my code that I couldn't see. After a night's sleep and a clear head, I usually had an epiphany when I woke up the next day and was able to fix whatever bugs I had. It was a pain in the ass! Tony had a friend named Chris Sealy who was a web developer. He worked on Nintendo's website so I knew that he knew his shit! I ran a test E3 site with him and he was able to convert my ideas into a smooth running CSS page in no time flat. This meant I was no longer going to go to sleep in tears over a bug I couldn't fix. I eventually made Tony the Senior Editor so he could deal with all the writers. It freed up time for me to do Davis Daily and other projects I was interested in. It was perfect. I had a long talk with him in the early stages of the site. I told him that we would bust our asses for 2 years straight and if the site didn't grow, I was going to retire. This was the last shot for me. So we busted our asses for two years, spawned a few more podcasts and did very good numbers. The growth of the site plateaued in the second year and I called it quits.

It seemed that with every website I built, I learned more and more about how it works. With vgt.com I didn't know what the fuck I was doing but it worked. With thebitbag.com, I got better at creating content and my first podcast became a hit. With stfuandplay.com I had a very clear and direct plan for success, but I couldn't pull it off. Once I was done with the site, it really started to dawn on my how much being a video game journalist sucks. In fact, it must suck more if you are actually running the site. When you are the publisher or editor in chief of a site, you have people to answer to. It's a job within a job. Many of my editors told me I was unapproachable and to this day I still don't understand why they felt this way. I was very open with all my ideas and wasn't mean to people, but I learned from my girlfriend that because I'm very headstrong and set in my ways, it makes me unapproachable. This is something that comes with running a site and delegating work to people. What I hated even worse was the fact that I wasn't paying people. The most I could ever do was pay for meals and get a huge hotel room for a bunch of us to crash in. There was the occasional advertising deal that came through but that went back into hosting fees and meals. Meanwhile Polygon got a $500,000 advertising deal with Microsoft when they LAUNCHED! It also dawned on me that you needed to have money to truly be successful. Every site that was successful started out with some kind of backing. We had nothing but the money in our pockets and our free time. We all had to work regular jobs and do most of our content creation at night. So what the fuck was I doing this for? I had been in the business since 1995 and had seen it all. There was nothing at any E3 that blew my mind anymore. In fact, E3 became a chore. Long flights to LA, at least $1500 in expenses and lots of work posting stories. On top of that I was burning my vacation time to do these shows. So when I came back from E3 tired as hell, I had to go right back to work. It sucked! A lot of my editors were having a ball doing E3 cuz they were new to it like I was in 1995. So I tried to be positive and not take away from their experience.

Torrence Davis(left) and Emilio Lopez(right) at E3 2013

While I may have had one of the best staff yet, in the back of my mind I realized that I hated running things. I had a vision and not many people understood it. We often debated about how the logo of the site should be changed. What they didn't realized is that I worked with Zack's Wife, Camile, for about a week to get the exact logo that I wanted. When it was finished and added to shirts and hats, the fans loved it! Even people who didn't know about the site loved the hats I made. I was creating a brand that was working, but the staff wanted to change it because they didn't like it. What they failed to understand is it's not about what we like, but about what our fans like. It's also about branding. That's why Coke and Pepsi still have the same colors and logo after all these years. Of all the things they should have been focusing on, I couldn't understand how changing the logo was a priority for them. It just goes to show that not everyone sees the big picture. As you become more experienced in whatever field you are in, the picture continues to grow bigger. If you can only see leaves in the picture, you'd have no idea that you were actually looking at a vista.

It became very clear to me that you can't make money in video game journalism. I mean, if you want to write about games for the rest of your life, you can get a paycheck and pay your bills and live happily ever after. However, do you just want to pay your bills or do you want to live comfortably? There's no true path in this business to being wealthy unless you can hit it big on Youtube. Print is dead and gaming websites are shit. Just go to any major website like IGN and you'll be bombarded with annoying advertising. These sites are run by huge fortune 500 companies that are owned by wealthy executives. Greg Miller, Jim Sterling and Colin Moriarty all figured it out. They left the website world and are now clearing 6 figures a year, doing the same thing they love in podcast and video form. They are making more money than they ever did at IGN and Destructoid.

After I announced the shutdown of the site, I encouraged editors to look for work with some of our friends. Tony Polanco went to thekoaltion.com. He brought Chris Sealy, Emilio Lopez, Brett Murdock and Rachel Murdock over with him. He also brought his podcasts, The Throwdown over to the site. I was happy for them and they were able to continue doing what they loved. The Throwdown is still going on strong today and has a secondary community driven podcast called Throwdown Your Questions.

Video Game Warzone

Sometime before I created The Bitbag, I was a co-host on a radio show in San Diego call 'Hot Set'. Hot Set was a talk show about film. My friend Bart scored some time at the radio station every Saturday and my friends Paul and Freddy and I were all part of this show. We had all attended film school together and helped work on each other's projects. If Bart was directing a film, I would help with titles and lighting, etc. If Paul directed, I was director of photography and maybe Freddy would assist with directing or other duties. We all helped each other out. Paul and I would occasionally have movie nights at our loft and that's where Bart proposed the idea to do the radio show. He had some contacts at this studio who was doing talk shows on the Internet called WTR(World Talk Radio). The network had a fully functional studio with a huge table, professional microphones, a glass window and old school mixing board. We would all head to the studio on Saturday afternoon to record our show. This was just when the podcasting boom was starting. I didn't know shit about podcasting, but WTR was treating it like a radio show but distributing it on the Internet. All we had to do was come up with content and show up and talk. Since we were film heads, it was easy and fun. I waited with baited breath every week for Saturday

to arrive. It was everything I lived for. I was
just a co-host but felt like a big celebrity
walking into that studio. We had a recording
engineer, a huge table with phat mics and
everything! I LOVED IT! We interviewed the
producer of Boondock Saints, Ricky Shroeder and
even Jimmy Gambina from Rocky fame! I don't know
how Bart had all these contacts but I was glad he
did. There was never a boring show! It all
ended one day during a taping of the show when
Bart, the host and creator, had a meltdown. I
can't quite remember why he blew up, but it was
funny as hell and it was on-air! That was our
very last show. We all continued to be friends
after the incident. Looking back on it, I think
it was just a disagreement we all had with Bart.
I had the radio bug after that and didn't know
what I was going to do with it. I wanted to get
back on the air so bad I could taste it!

    After I had started The Bitbag, I moved back
home to Boston. Once I got everything setup, I
started to look into this thing called
podcasting. It was basically talk radio for the
Internet and it was amazing! I did a ton of
research on how and where to host the files and
then had to decide how I was going to record it.
At the time, Skype seemed like the perfect tool.
You could have a bunch of people in the room at
one time and using a digital audio workstation,
you could record and then edit the conversation.
I decided to get a bunch of editors from my site
together and start recording. I had Lee Yi, John
Sitzman and a few others join in from time to
time. Even Perry Mercer did an episode with us.
At the time I also hired a writer to add a
woman's touch to the site. I thought that a
woman's gaming point of view was something that
was missing in the industry. The girl I brought
on, although she seemed like she knew her stuff,
ended up being a hypochondriac that would only
talk about her pain and always brought up stories
about her father. It was nauseating. I

eventually canceled that podcast because it really wasn't what I wanted, but I got my feet wet. But hey, I was podcasting right?!

Candid Anthony was very outspoken and comical. He has a personality that is just fun to witness. We were in the car running some errands one day and he was explaining to me why he returned his PS3 copy of Assassin's Creed for the Xbox 360 version. It basically came down to him hunting these hidden flags and not getting an Achievement for it. Achievements were very important to him and he wasn't going to waste hours of time doing all the work without getting anything in return for it. I recorded this conversation and posted it on bliptv and also on N4G. Hiphopgamer caught wind of this video and created a response video and a rap to go with it. It was hilarious! I got in touch with him and we talked for about 2 hours. The conversation was all about gaming and we debated many different things about the games we loved. It was so good I told him that we should have recorded it. He agreed with me and we decided to make it a weekly conversation and call it the Warzone!

When I think of the early days of the Warzone, it reminds me of a bunch of gamers getting together in a living room to talk video games. That's basically what it was. It had started with just Hiphopgamer and I and then I started doing it live on Skype. People could come in and listen and even ask questions. Skype was a horrible platform for this though as it didn't allow me any flexibility. I then switched to Teamspeak. Teamspeak allowed me to moderate the room, chat with text, ban and kick people, post links and send private messages all during the live broadcast. It also allowed me a larger room capacity. I can remember at one time the entire room filled up with 50 people and I couldn't log in to do the show. Someone had to leave so I could get in. I boosted the cap to 75 people to fix that problem.

The Warzone was an uncontrollable beast that I had created due to my love of radio. Before I knew it, I was getting emails from all over the world telling me how much they loved my show. One guy said he would listen to the long format show on his way to sing in the Opera. He would drive 2 hours on the Autobahn in Germany to get to work and it was my show that kept him entertained during the trip. There are people who listened to the show throughout their entire college career. I knew what I had but then again I didn't. I had a lot of black and Latino followers. I never marketed myself as a 'black' podcast host, but once people saw what I looked like, they were happy to know that they could relate to me. My fans ranged from teenagers to men in their late 40's. There are even a few women who tune in every week for my dick and fart type humor based on video games. I'm always amazed at the power of fans. When I had fans asking for my picture and my autograph at New York Comic Con, I was beside myself. I really didn't know how to handle this tiny bit of fame I had, but I was very humble. It was this very reason why I still to this day do the show for my fans! They are the reason I've kept going all these years.

At some point during my career, I DID cancel the Warzone due to the fact that the show had gone completely out of control. Hiphopgamer was going places with his career and was frequently a no-show. This really wasn't an issue because I had plenty of voices giving input during the show. However, giving freedom to too many voices, especially to fans, grew out of control. Everyone had something to say and usually had to talk over each other to make their point. This was also the case with Hiphopgamer. The chaos reached a point where I couldn't even make my points and I was the host of the show. I started thinking about canceling the show and mentioned it to a few people. Jagon came on the show, like

me usually did, and asked me about this rumor
that I was canceling. Right after he questioned
me about it I said, "Yes, this is the last
episode of the Warzone. Batman Motherfucker"! I
ended it and that was that. I knew what I had
but at the time was not happy about what it
turned into. I still loved radio but I think
leaving the show and recharging my batteries was
a good thing. I got tons of requests to bring
the Warzone back. People would hit me up on
Twitter constantly asking for the show to come
back. About a year later I brought it back with
a force! I did a Patreon to bring some money in
to help pay for hosting fees and also to help
purchase prizes for contests. I stuck with the 2
hour format for the most part and changed a few
other things around. I was the main host with
Zack Warren as my co-host and Cueil, Shaz and
Freddy offering input here and there. Then of
course we'd occasionally have that crazy
Canadian, Megajack, on the show too! I made
sure that only one person got the mic at a time.
This way everyone got a chance to be heard. Loud
arguments turned into mature debates and I
started giving away games more frequently. The
hardest part about returning was getting all
those old fans back. STFUandPlay wasn't being
updated anymore so if they didn't follow the RSS
or iTunes feed, they wouldn't know we were back.
I slowly started getting old fans back here and
there over the first year of the return of the
show.
        I also had a second podcast called The
Morning Gamer. After I left my job at Harvard
Law School in March of 2012, I didn't work for
like 8 months. I still did the Warzone but when
I decided to spend about a month in the West
Coast, I needed a way to stay in touch with my
fans. So I would wake up early every day and
just babble about games and tech and called the
show The Morning Gamer. It was an instant hit
with my fans and a break away from the craziness

that was the Warzone. It was just me, solo on
the mic like a typical morning talk show. I
still love the format and still infrequently put
out a show here and there depending on what's
going on in the industry.

State Of The Industry

I wasn't happy with the state of the industry. Polygon went straight Polygoon and focused on sexism in video games and other controversial bullshit that no real gamer cared about. It's almost like Polygon was a trojan horse and it was a huge white knight filled with SJW(Social Justice Warriors). Whatever they were doing was spreading to other sites too. Kotaku became nothing but a fishwrap tabloid site. Not only did they twist words that were said in interviews to create more clickbait, they also followed the trend of focusing on sexism in games. Adam Sessler, a man I used to respect, published a video review on God Of War Ascension. While most of the review focused on the game, he made a huge fuss about a trophy called "Bros Before Hoes". Either he's been living under a rock and never heard it before or he was just jumping on the SJW bandwagon. You'd get the trophy after defeating some ugly creature from hell who happened to be female, but wasn't human. Because of his antics, Sony Santa Monica did an update to the game CHANGING the name of the trophy to "Bros Before Foes". I mean seriously, WHAT THE FUCK!? So fuck Adam for making a big deal about it in a game where not only 1000's of men get brutally murdered, but women are also either killed or used for mini-sex games. I was

done with him and highly pissed at Sony Santa
Monica for changing it. I didn't update my PS3
for a month just so I could have the original
trophy on my profile.

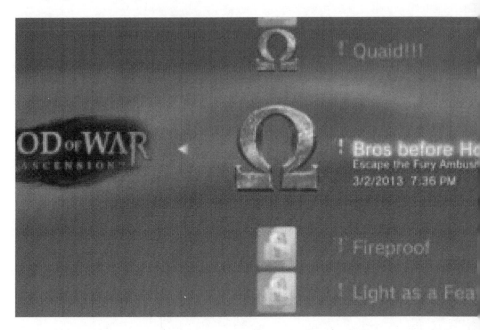

     Sites were closed down like crazy. Joystiq
and Gametrailers closed down, Bitmob was bought
by Venture Beat and Giant Bomb moved back to
Gamespot. So if sites that were making money
were going under, what in the hell could I do
with a site. How could I stay afloat and make a
money earning career out of doing game sites? I
couldn't. The news reporting part of the
industry was changing. Traditional game sites
were being looked over due to the increase of
popular YouTube channels. YouTubers had video of
the games they were playing right when they were
released. If they weren't playing them on
release day, they were getting the games early
and posting the footage before any site could.
YouTubers and streamers were making millions of
dollars. Even if you didn't know shit about
video games, as long as you had tits and showed

cleavage, you could make enough money to pay all your bills, buy your equipment and travel. These people were making a new type of career out of gaming. It was amazing! Jim Sterling left Destructoid and started a Patreon for Jimquisition, his video review show. He's making $10,239 a month! I started a Patreon for Video Game Warzone. I mean why not right? I'm clearing a staggering $42 a month. Jim is fatter than me so I know it's not my weight. Maybe I need to speak with an English accent? I don't know because there is no formula to success when it comes to making games content.

Another thing that I hated about this industry was the fact that publishers were using lazy methods to determine who they wanted to support. It was hard enough generating enough traffic to please the publishers, but now we had to be a part of this site called Metacritic. Metacritic is an aggregate site that takes user and press reviews to generate an average score for a game. Since publishers depended on high scores to sell more games, they wanted outlets to be a member of the Metacritic site before they would support them with review materials and access. It was pure bullshit! While it was true that games with higher scores sold more copies, it had nothing to do with the relationship between the press outlet and the publisher. If you were a site that didn't have scores for reviews, you couldn't become a part of Metacritic. Even if you DID put scores in your reviews, there was a chance Metacritic might not approve you as an outlet in their scoring matrix. What pissed me off even more is that Metacritic was allowing publishers to determine press access based on their Metacritic membership. If I ran Metacritic I would threaten to remove all past and future scores of said publishers games off of the site if they continued to do this. Imagine if you couldn't get press access if you weren't a member of another press site? The other thing

about Metacritic is that they were encouraging
hungry sites to continue using scores for their
games. It was a never ending cycle of bullshit
and it set Metacritic up to be successful based
on the publishers need for their scores.

   After the God Of War Ascension fiasco, I
thought that I had seen everything. Just
recently, a gamer was playing Watch Dogs 2 and
accidentally killed a prostitute. As she lied
dead on the ground, her panties were exposed. As
she was a prostitute, she had crotchless panties
and an anatomically correct vagina with pubic
hair and all the trimmings. This, as far as I
know, was a first for gaming! The fact that
Ubisoft decided to put this much detail into
their NPC(Non-Player Character) characters was
great! It's an M rated game so all bets are off.
It turns out that the gamer who found this,
posted a picture of it and Sony, following
policy, banned him for posting lewd content.
This however, was IN GAME content and he had
every right to post it. Sony later removed the
ban, but due to the controversy of this pic,
Ubisoft removed crotchless panties from their
prostitute NPCs and put clothes on every nude bum
in the game. Why are publishers censoring M
rated games AFTER they get approved for release?
This is the gaming industry. You'd never see
this done in film, comics, books or music. Only
in a video game do you see a publisher remove one
of the things that made the game M rated in the
first place. It's ludicrous to even think about
it, but this is the industry that I've been in
for years. It's changed thanks to social media
and every one having an opinion. So in essence,
giving gamers and the press a voice, has led us
to censoring the things we love to see in games.
Art imitates life, but that's not even the case
anymore. Art can be subjected to censorship
regardless of who its made for. It's a true
insult to the intelligence of the adult consumers
purchasing games for their entertainment.

Where Am I Now

Today is April 4, 2017. This is the last chapter of my book. I'm sitting here with a smile on my face knowing that I'm about to complete yet another project. Life is wonderful. I've always thought that if you are going to live a life on this planet, create something. Leave something behind for others to read, listen to or watch. Make your mark because once you're gone, that's it! The creative engine ceases to exist and you become history. Do you have a legacy or don't you? I know that when I'm on my death bed I want to look back on my life and feel accomplished. That's why I've done so many different things. I'm a filmmaker, photographer, writer, artist and podcast personality. I love to create and that, plus my love for video games, is ultimately what motivated me to become a video game journalist.

Maybe your story will be different. Maybe you've already started a blog and one little tip in this book helped you get over a hump. Maybe you're an accomplished game journalist and you can relate to some of the things I've written about. I hope that it's educational, enlightening and entertaining. I want you to be inspired just like I was when I read Rebel Without A Crew by Robert Rodriguez. I was so inspired by that book that I adapted the title.

A little inspiration is all we need. When I was young, magazines like EGM, Next Generation and Diehard Gamefan all inspired me. I thought it would be so cool to one day get free games for review so I could inform the world just how awesome they were. In the end, I made that dream come true.

The dream is still alive. Today I'm inspired by social media and Youtube. I used to think Youtube wasn't a sure shot. There is no formula to success. It takes one viral video and then you blow up. But that's not really true. Youtube is like a really huge television network. If you want to be successful you have to be dedicated and make content people want to watch. Marques Brownlee is one of my inspirations on Youtube. It's not what he does that impresses me, but how he does it. Tech has always been something I love to do and no matter how much I try to get away from it, I'm always drawn back into it. I created a new site called Tekiyo, but it's been stagnant for a few years. I've decided that it's best to move Tekiyo to an all video channel on Youtube. I've been researching and acquiring new equipment to start doing video reviews on a regular basis. While I have many tech contacts in the business, it's easier for me to procure the tech that I love myself and just review it. That's what passion is all about. I do it for the love of tech, not to get free stuff!

I've also run into some accidental success with my other Youtube channel called Bubba Bass Anglers. At first it was just a place for me to post videos of my fishing adventures with my friends. I never took it seriously and it was more of a record of what we caught and funny stuff that happened while out on the water. 2 years after launching the site, lure manufacturers are sending me their fishing products to review. I'm using my expertise of product reviewing for the fishing channel and it's working. It actually gives me the edge among some of the more popular fishing channels because they don't do reviews.

The Video Game Warzone is still alive and kicking. As of this writing I have just recorded episode #315. It's available on vgwarzone.com and also on Youtube. I don't think I'll ever stop doing the Warzone again. Quitting the show that one time allowed me to make it the better show it is today. I'm very pleased with it now and it can only get bigger. I'm dabbling into paid marketing to push my content further out there and it's working. You gotta spend money to make money!

Gaming has always been a passion of mine and I'll definitely be gaming until I'm dead. While I love gaming and it's a major hobby of mine, I'm finding that there are so many other more important things for me to do in life. I remember when I was young and had no responsibilities, gaming was everything. I could play games all hours of the day and night without a care. I can't do that anymore and I really don't want to. I look at some guys in my community and I just shake my head at how much they prioritize everything gaming. I often wonder if they have anything else going on in life or is gaming it!? I think my fans appreciate my knowledge and experience but at the same time have to understand that gaming is never going to get the focus that I used to give it. My back log is for life! I truly wish I could take time to finish most of my games, but I won't be able to do it for a long time. I'm also not buying games as much as I used to. I'd rather spend the money on photo equipment, tech and fishing gear. This doesn't mean my head still isn't in the game industry, because it is and always will be. I know that when most of my younger fans get my age, they'll understand. You only live once, so get it done while you're here!

The 10 Minute Video Game

Journalism School

Learn To Write...Or Talk

If you want to make it in journalism, you have to learn how to write. It's just like being a carpenter. If you can't use a hammer, you are useless and won't get any work. The same applies to video game journalism. While there are people that don't take it seriously, us game journalist do. That means your reviews, previews and editorials have to capture the reader. I'll be honest here, if your grammar sucks, but you can write something interesting, you've still won. There's a reason they have copy editors right? A copy editor might be one boring ass writer, but they kick ass at finding your mistakes and cleaning everything up. Writing is a skill. You get better with practice, but that doesn't mean that you'll be good at it. For example, you may know how to play basketball very well, but that doesn't mean you're a Michael Jordan. If you're good enough, they'll pick you for the team though. So the first thing you must do to become a good journalist is write your ass off.

I was never a big book reader. I read short children's books as a kid, but when I got older I had no interest in novels. Well, I have an interest, but I don't like spending time reading novels…even good ones. Reference and non-fiction books are my poison. I love listening to the perspective of the author. A lot of times I can either relate to them or learn from them. I can't get that from reading a 300 page novel. One of my favorite non-fiction reads is "Rebel Without A Crew" by Robert Rodriguez. I'm a filmmaker and this book was just a joy to read. He wrote about his journey from wannabe filmmaker to Hollywood success. He detailed everything from budgeting all the way to playing his film at festivals. The writing style inspired me to write this book, Rebel Without A Pause Button.

I didn't really get interested in writing until I was well into high school. Most of the writing I did back then was boring book reports. They had us writing book reports on some of the most boring reads in history like Great Expectations. I got to chapter 42 before I quit reading that book. I bought the Cliff Notes and still failed the exam. It sucked so bad! I don't even know why they made us do book reports. What were we actually learning from English Literature? An even better question was why were they forcing us to take this course, but not forcing us to take African Studies? At some point I started writing game reviews back and forth with my cousin. That was fun and it was a great exercise to prep me for the future. I also had an interest in story telling, but with film, not with paper. After my cousin and I had gone to Ft. Lauderdale for spring break, I started hand writing a story of all our adventures called "Perry And Torrence's Wild Adventures". I never finished the story but kept writing reviews. When I got into college, my English professor made us write in a journal. I always thought that if I wanted to keep a journal, it would be something personal. So why was my English professor making me write in a journal if she wasn't supposed to be reading it? I started writing porn in my journal to entertain myself. I thought she wasn't reading it so what did it matter if I was writing porn? I turned in my journal and thought nothing of it. The next day she returned all the journals back to us and mine had a big red D with a little note written in it. She said, "If you are going to write porn, at least make it interesting". I was in shock and super embarrassed. I couldn't even look at her for the rest of the class. I couldn't help but think that she must think I'm some weirdo or pervert. This whole thing backfired, but I decided to listen to her and make it interesting next time. I went home and wrote romantic encounters in my journal. It was still all fiction, but I made it interesting. It was like what women were reading in those old Harlequin novels. It was classy, erotic, mature and well written. I proudly handed my journal in to her and when she returned it, I no longer had anything to be embarrassed about. She gave me an "A-" and noted how it kept her interest this time. This was an important lesson for me. It taught me that if the reader was interested in the story, they'll enjoy it. If you bore the reader, they'll probably never want to read anything from you again.

So where do you learn how to write? Well, a lot of publications would prefer if you learned the AP style of writing. I've looked at it and may even use some of it, but as I've said, practice makes perfect. The AP (Associated Press) Style Guide will teach you some things you probably don't know like the serial comma, how and when to capitalize and how to use colons. It's a great reference guide and may help in your journey to become a better writer. I've looked at the AP Style Guide a few times, but it's not something I depend on or follow religiously. Like I've said, before you become an expert at grammar, learn how to capture your audience with writing that pulls the reader in and keeps them wanting more.

Back in the days of video game magazines, if you knew how to write, that's all you needed to be successful. I can't say the same for 2017.

We are in the Youtube age and you must acquire many skills to become a great journalist. One of those skills is learning how to talk. If you can talk, you can do a podcast or video series. A podcast is talking in front of a microphone, a video is talking in front of a camera. If you're camera and/or mic shy, you'll never be able to deliver your message because you'll be too busy focusing on your nerves. In order to learn how to talk, like writing, you must practice it. You can start by doing the most simple of things, create a podcast. I don't care what your podcast about, just create one and produce it weekly. I love radio, but I've always loved to run my mouth and entertain my friends. It made it natural for me to transition into podcasting and video. For the most part, I'm not doing anything different than I did over my cousin's house or on the bus ride to school. I used to tell my friends how awesome some of the video games I was playing were. It was so much a part of my childhood that it became intrinsic to my personality. This would later fuel my love for podcasting and video production.

Random Editorials From The Past

Writing editorials is the perfect writing practice. It gives you the opportunity to speak your mind on a subject and enlighten your audience. Back in the day, reading an editorial was the first thing you did before reading any other content in a magazine. It was the first bit of content you would see. I've enclosed some very old editorials I wrote for vgt.com. I think you'll find some of the ideas that I discussed very interesting. I've decided not to edit these editorials so you can read it as it was posted.

VGT.COM
1997

There's been a lot of stuff happening in the gaming industry as of late. Nintendo is planning on dropping the price of the N64, Sony has already dropped the Playstation down to $149, and Sega is selling more and more Saturns due to it's 3 free games deal. On top of that, we are all in store for a hell of year, even better than last year.

This great industry isn't without it's

problems. I still see punks posting messages on
the Usenet like "Sega Suks", "Sony Stinks", and
"Nintendo Blows", and it really amazes me.
Numerous counts of bias still remains in
magazines and other gaming sites. It seems that
this will not cease. If your a gamer looking for
straightforward information, you know what
sources you can count on. Just enjoy the games
and be happy. The one thing that still pisses me
off is lazy programmers. If you Saturn owners are
always wondering why the the original Playstation
versions of games are better than the Saturn
versions, it's because of lazy programming. After
seeing what AM2, AM3, Scavenger, Core, and EA can
do, there's no excuse for sloppy ports. I
especially have to commend EA on the wonderful
job they've done. All of their Saturn ports of
Playstation games are exact. I must make a note
that Probe's conversion of Diehard Trilogy is
excellent. With the exception of the handling on
Die Hard With A Vengeance, the game is just as
good as the Playstation version. All of these
things I'm discussing here are important, not
only to properly inform you, but also to kill
these rumors that are being spread by bias
editors and miscellaneous geeks on the net.

Now for a little bit on E3. As always, we
are gearing up for E3 '97. We are trying to get
as much information as we can to do a little E3
preview of all of the games that will be at the
show. Keep checking our site as we will be
leaking out as much info as we can on all of the
new titles and surprises that are in store at
this years E3. As for the next E3 video, we are
planning to put 3 hours of footage on tape this
time around. We'll try to get as much footage as
we can of the "behind closed doors" stuff. That's
what everyone wants to see isn't it?

As you can see a lot of changes have been
done to our web page. We've redone some graphics
and started working on our PC Gaming section. We
will have a ton of demo's available, as well as

previews, news, and movie clips. We are growing and are still in need of a few writers for Anime Extra, PC Gaming, and Kung Fu Theater. Send all inquiries to: Editor In Chief.

I'm really good at making predictions about the video game industry, so I made a list of things that I think are going happen towards the end of this year and at E3.

E3:

1) Sega drops Saturn down to $149 and includes one game to compete with Sony.

2) Nintendo has a prototype 64DD running Zelda.

3) Core should have early Tomb Raider 2 shots up and running

4) Sega with have the finished "Model 3" emulator for the Saturn running a demo showing it's power of 1 million polys per second.

5) Capcom will have Marvel Super Heroes, D&D, and SF vs Xmen. Also Cyberbots with RAM Cart. Resident Evil 2 will be shown in early form too.

6) We'll see more 3rd party titles for Saturn than before.

7) Panzer Dragoon 3 surprise? Maybe

8) Sonic Xtreme? Definitely

9) M2... Possibly with running demos and D2 or Enemy Zero running.

10) Final Fantasy VII for Playstation will be up and running.

11) Grandia will be in form for the Saturn

12) Sega will outdo themselves and have the best party ever.

This year:

1) Nintendo will release 64DD for $150 and leave the public dazed and confused.

2) Nintendo will if not already drop the 64 down to $149 to compete with Sony and Sega.

3) As promising as the 64DD looks, sales will be slow.

4) Namco will announce that they will be

doing games for the Saturn (once the upgrade gets finished)

5) Core will announce Tomb Raider 2 for Saturn, Saturn upgrade, and PSX.

6) Sony will release official specs on Playstation 2, after Christmas.

7) Someone, probably AM2, will max out the Saturns capabilities and astound everyone.

Torrence Davis

Editor In Chief

Notice to Web Sites:

IF YOU GET IT FROM THIS PAGE, PLEASE CREDIT US!

1998

Is Sega Ready For The Next Round?

There has been a lot of talk about Sega and their unannounced super system; the Katana. Sega seems to have given up on their present 32bit Saturn system and has been talking to developers about producing games for their 64bit system. So what's going to happen to the Saturn and how will their owners respond to another Sega system dumped by the waist side? It was not too long ago when Sega was the top dog in the gaming industry. They were reaping the rewards for best game console and advertisement. Now those days are gone and Sega is making one last ditch effort to scale the mountain and become the #1 player is the gaming business. So how do they get there? Better yet, how do they stay there? This is my focus for this editorial.

Let's get one thing straight right from the start. The Saturn is basically dead. There is no chance for this system to all of a sudden start selling and gaining a large share of the market. It's not going to happen. Yes, there are a lot of decent software out there for the system, but because most retailers are ditching the system and slashing the prices on software, we can expect the selection of games to be minimal. Therefore purchasing the system is not recommended at this time. Expect the system to drop to $99 at next year's E3 and the software to drop even further. Next year will be the last hurrah for the Saturn so all owners of this system should grab up the cheap software as soon as they see it. O.k., enough on the Saturn. Let's talk about Sega's future system, "The Kitana".

So far Sega is doing everything right in getting this system prepared. They have three major companies to give them the support, technology and marketing power to lift them back into the race. These companies are Microsoft, Hitachi, & NEC. At this point in time NEC & Sega are working extremely hard trying to get third-party companies to sign on to develope for their new system. NEC is expressing the power of their VR Power chipset and Sega is promising that the OS, CPU, development tools, RAM, graphics, sound and all around power of the system will be much better than their ill-fated Saturn. The marketing ploy seems to be working so far since companies like Activision, Acclaim, Shiny Entertainment, Capcom, EA, and many other have expressed interests in producing games for the system. Even though many developers are eager to make the jump to the new system, most will probably wait for the user base to build up before reaching for a development kit. Companies that do decide to make games will probably only develop one or two and see how well they sell. Because Sega's last three systems (Sega CD, 32X, & Saturn) have all bombed out before their time, gamers are not so eager to grab the next system that Sega produces. After reading many e-mails and the newgroup postings, I've notice many Sega fans to be disappointed in SOA efforts to support the Saturn. Even SOJ has recently showed their anger at the SOA executives and their lack of a marketing strategy. Here's what Sega must do to be successful with their new system and capture back the market they possessed previously.

1) Hype Their New 64bit System: Nintendo is famous for doing this. They'll leak just enough info to get gamers excited and then delay their system for 2 years. Seriously though, Sega needs to get us gamers interested in their hardware now. They need to keep feeding us some good info about the what makes up the system, the games the will be played on it, the developers who have signed on, the price, and a tentative date of release. All of this is extremely important to us and Sega's well being.

2) Continue To Support The Saturn: Many gamers may ask, "Why bother?" By supporting their current system it help to keep a link to their loyal fans. Even if third party companies have ditch the Saturn, Sega must continue to produce games until the new system is released. Saturn owners will know that Sega hasn't deserted them and it turn will keep the faith. Sega should really get some import games over here, since many of those games are truly incredible. There are enough decent import games in Japan to give Saturn fans happy until the new system is released.

3) Make The 64bit System Backward Compatible: Of course Sega has already stated that the system would not be backward compatible, but it really should be. People don't like to have two, three or even four systems hooked up to one T.V. (I have this crazy hook up, so I know.) By having this compatibility Sega can support the Saturn a little longer until gamers upgrade. Sega could also continue to sell some of their older Saturn games to people who never purchased a Saturn. Of course the main reason is, we don't have to switch cables to play our favorite Saturn game.

4) Keep The Price Under $250: When the 3DO was launched it retailed for an amazing $699.99. Many rich gamers rushed out and purchased the system only to find the price drop six months later. Another six months it dropped again to under $300 and started selling like crazy. Angry gamers who purchased the system first wanted a refund difference from 3DO, but of course that never happened. Because Sega has dragged their systems into the ground more then once, gamers are now aware of Sega's trend and won't get burned again. If Sega launches their system for more than $400.00 the sales will not even match the Jaguar's launch. If they can get it under $250, and market it accordingly, the user base will grow.

5) More Than 15 Games Ready At Launch Time: When Sega released their Saturn system they had exactly 6 games ready to play. I know this because Sega gave us the 6 games the day of the launch. Six games were not nearly enough and the quality of the games weren't what gamers expected. Nintendo says that the quality of the games will sell systems. This is true, but having good quality and quantity will sell more. Sega must have at least 10 sure fire hits when the Kitana is released. Gamers are looking for VF3, Daytona 2, Super GT, The Lost World, and other arcade hits. They're also should be a good amount of third-party titles as well. Each title should exhibit what the hardware and development tools can do. If they can impress the gamers and developers at launch time they will succeed.

6) Prepare An Awesome Marketing & Advertising Campaign: This is a must. With Microsoft, NEC & Hitachi backing Sega on their system they shouldn't have a problem getting the info on T.V., in magazines & newspapers, on billboards, on the radio, at retail stores, and in the gamer's brains. Everyone will need to know just how great this 64bit system is and what it can do to entertain us. This expensive campaign should start at the E3 and build up until the launch date.

I feel that Sega can get back into the race, but they have to remember what got them there the first time and got back to that strategy to be successful. Sony did everything right when they launched their system. The timing was perfect and the hardware and games lived up to the hype. Even though there were some minor overheating problems with the system, most gamers found solutions to the problem and continued to support Sony's wonder machine.

E-Mail the Editor at pmercer@vgt.com

The Ideal Gaming System

Lately we've been hearing alot about Sega's new "Dural","Blackbelt","Katana" system. I have mixed feelings about it myself. Why do we need another system? I mean, we do need another system, but only one more. This video gaming war has got me going crazy. You should see my desk. I have two Playstations, a Saturn with import card, Sega Genesis, Sega CD, SNES, and an Nintendo 64. This is all on my desk! Anyways, like I said in one of my other videtorials, I really want a system that's capable of playing Model 3 type games. Sega's new system will probably do this. But then I'm going to have to buy the Playstation 2, and then probably the Nintendo 128. I can't stand this anymore! Why can't we just have one system???

Now there's some speculation as to whether Sega is going to get out of the hardware race altogether, and become a software only company. That would give them endless routes to take in gaming development.This would be to their best interest as far as I'm concerned. Imagine Sega publishing games on the PSX?? Wouldn't that be great??? No, I don't think so. Maybe the PSX2 would be a great area for them to start cross development on, but not the current Playstation. So what is my theory of the ideal gaming system?? Let's take a look at two possible scenarios here. 1) Sega and NEC make the Katana and NEC takes over all hardware responsibilities, while Sega does software only. NEC recruits all of the great third parties, and we have the gaming solution of the century. Then comes the PSX2. 2) The Playstation 2 hits the shelves and Nintendo completely loses the video game race. Sega and all of Sega's third parties start developing games for the PSX2. Everyone realizes it's THE system of choice, and it becomes the only game system on the market. There's our one system solution. I'll have one box that plays all of my favorite games. I'll have no crazy decisions to make during Xmas season because there is only ONE system. All the great games I want to play will be available for ONE system. It will have the ultimate sprite engine, and the surpreme 3D engine. It will play games like Street Fighter III and Virtua Fighter 3 EXACTLY like the arcade. It will have a CD-ROM and a Memory Card slot. I'll be able to buy games from Namco, Sega, Sony, and probably Nintendo for my one black box.

Well, this is my theory. I hope something like this really happens because I'm sick of the system wars. Why don't you send me an email telling me what you think the ideal game system is.

E-Mail the Editor at tdavis@vgt.com
Torrence Davis
Editor In Chief

2000

Wrestling Games

I'd like to take this time to write about the state of wrestling games for all console systems. As we all know, the popularity of the WCW, WWF, and ECW is at an all time high. The result, as with anything that is popular at the moment, is the production of all sorts of games trying to find success from the wrestling craze. However, not one of the wrestling games released in the states is worth more than about 2 seconds of rental time.

Every single wrestling game brought out here for the 'next gen' systems have a few traits that don't change no matter what company makes it or what system it's released for. One thing is the game being polygonal...first mistake. Polygons don't mean squat to me. So what if that's the way things are going? So what if that's considered the future of gaming. With certain types of games, polygons just do not work. Everything looks robotic and entirely fake (no pun intended). From walking to running to doing some type of move, these games just are horribly jerky and look nothing at all like what you see on TV. Sprite based wrestling games just 'feel' and play better, just take a look back to Tecmo Wrestling or Pro Wrestling or even Mat Mania. Those games were fun, fast, and drawn very well. Polygons do not have a place in every single genre. The only series of polygonal wrestling games that were any good were the All Japan Pro Wrestling series for Playstation, Saturn, and Dreamcast; by the way, not released in America to keep that trend of lame wrestling games alive here. They all played pretty well, but were not as fast or as responsive as a sprite based wrestler. This is

just something that won't change no matter how
many polygons you squeeze on the screen. The very
best wrestling series, Fire Pro, has been around
for about a decade and it's sprite based. It's
the most fun, realistic, fast paced, best drawn,
playable bunch of wrestling games ever made.
Again, though, none of the series was released
here mainly due to licensing problems.

Another problem with U.S. wrestling games is
the control and the 'same move for each guy
besides the finisher' syndrome. Why are all these
games coming out based on doing some type of
combo to perform a suplex? That is the most
ridiculous thing I've ever heard, not to mention
it severely dampens the overall fun factor. "I
pushed up, triangle, left, square, but forgot to
hold R2...so I missed that body slam." What's up
with that? That's the only thing that keeps the
All Japan Pro Series from being fun. Fire Pro is
set on a one button mode. You time the press
right, you do the move if your opponent is worn
down. Even if you time it right, it can be
blocked or reversed. This system isn't easy to
learn when compared to games like Wrestlefest
where whomever pounds the button fastest, wins,
but is much more enjoyable than doing some stupid
combination of buttons. Perhaps the next Fire Pro
could have an option to choose between one button
and button mashing mode. Are you listening,
Human? Anyhow, that control issue is another
negative of these WCW Thunder and WWF Attitude
games. Programming all the wrestlers to do the
same exact moves is also horrible. Not every
single person does a power bomb or a suplex and
so on. Look again toward the Japanese wrestlers.
Each wrestler has his own set of moves which is
generally unique aside from the basic body slam
and maybe a suplex. Firepro, where each wrestler
has about 50 moves from a list of around 300 plus
total moves, allows each wrestler's true likeness
to be expressed. There are variations to suplexes

and body slams, as well as the specialties and finishers. You turn the TV on any night and you can be guaranteed each wrestler will NOT do the same moves as the next. Plain and simple, the American games need to add variety to each wrestler..which is a trend that seems to be finally catching on.

Yet another flaw in ALL wrestling games is the fact that you can have a guy like Rey Misterio powerbomb someone like the Giant (back when he was in WCW). Since just about every American wrestling game doesn't even take into account the wear down factor before doing more damaging moves, this is painfully evident. There has to be some way to code each wrestler to not have the ability to do certain moves against a much larger foe. It's all about common sense. On the same note as a small guy powerbombing a huge guy, it's equally ridiculous for a big guy to do top rope moves or head scissors type moves. Admittedly, even Fire Pro falls in this area, though it is much harder to actually pull the move off if your guy is smaller (you have to get real lucky and have the opponent really worn down). This is just one area ALL wrestling games can be improved in, it's just common sense everyone!

All this boils down to is fun. American wrestling games are not fun because they have Stone Cold or Hogan along with their theme music and little intro movie. It's not because they can do their finishing moves. It's not because they are robotic, non motion captured, stiff, jagged polygonal people moving like snails around a ring surrounded by a cardboard cut-out crowd. Easy control, easy execution, variety in moves and realism based on each personality, tons of options, battle royals, well drawn wrestlers/moves AND settings (including crowd), and being able to create your own wrestler/make ones not readily available in game exactly as you want in appearance and moves.

Please read my review of Fire Pro for Saturn and my upcoming review of Fire Pro G for Playstation to see how the REAL wrestling games stack up and what they need to improve on. As they are, though, they are leaps and bounds ahead of any American wrestling game..Acclaim and THQ can't do it right..they should have thrown in the towel long ago. EA might have something with their Mayhem title, but for now and since '89, Human has the title for making the best wrestling games, even if they never made it out here in the US. Import gaming is the key folks, get into it and you will be happy. Adapters for Playstation and Saturn really aren't that expensive. If you want the best in terms of quality and quantity, not to mention wrestling fun, take a look at either Fire Pro S for Saturn or Fire Pro G for Playstation. Translation guides are abundant and the fun is unlimited with these games.

Thanks for reading and feel free to send me your comments and questions! Thanks again for your support!

Matt Jenkins - Associate Editor

2001

Sony's Hype machine and the ones who believed the hype

Before you slam my email with words of hate and discontent, let me tell you that I think the PS2 is a marvelous system and I can't wait to get my hands on one. Well really, I CAN wait. And that's what this videtorial is all about.

You have 3 different sets of gamers out there. Hardcore true gamers like myself, fanboys, and casual gamers. True gamers will buy any and all game systems that come out, just to have the chance to play cool games. For example, most true gamers probably went out and bought a Neo Geo Pocket Color. I did. Most true gamers probably own Playstation, Sega Saturn, Nintendo 64 and all the old 16 and 8-bit systems. Fanboys only buy systems and games from one company. Fanboys will tell you Shenmue is crappy just because it's not on their system. Fanboys will tell you that the PS2 sucks because of the "jaggies". Lastly, casual gamers are the people who buy games and systems based on what there friends and commercials tell them. Casual gamers have no mind of their own and will own a system just so they can say that they have it. What ever is popular at the time will be prey for the casual gamer. Once a casual gamer has a system, they might buy 7 - 10 games for it in it's life time. On top of that, those 7-10 games were either REALLY popular or recommended by friends.

Sony's marketing machine worked for all 3 types of gamers. These 3 types of gamers who bought the system on launch date are called "early adopters". Now let me tell you this, the ONLY reason why I didn't fit into the early

adopter category is because of price. To me,
unless you have money to burn, $299.00 is too
much to pay for a gaming system. All my fellow
editors, who are true gamers themselves, agree
with me. It's just too much. Why couldn't Sony
have released it without DVD movie playback? They
could've released it without the MPEG2 Decoder
but with the DVD drive intact. I don't think any
of the DVD games are utilizing the decoder. They
are just using the high capacity discs to store
data as you would on a PC DVD drive. This would
have given them the excuse to drop the price down
to $199.00 and really compete with Sega. But Sony
wants the PS2 to be the future of entertainment.
Please. Spare me the bullshit and give me the
games.

What about the Dreamcast? Do people still
have no faith in Sega? The retailers do. I was
surprised to hear on clerk at Software Etc.
comment on Madden 2001 when asked if it was
better than NFL2K1. He said they were about the
same. Which is true. They are different games but
as far as gameplay and quality, they are about
the same. And don't forget that the Dreamcast
games look just as good as PS2 games as a
whole.But why aren't some people buying
Dreamcast? Why didn't Sega get all the attention
that Sony is getting during the Dreamcast launch
last year? Why are there still some IDIOTS out
there who think Dreamcast is just gonna go away
now that the PS2 is out!?!?!?

So I've made a choice. Should I pay $600 and
get 2 PS2's and sell one on ebay to make all of
my money back? Should I just get one PS2 because
I love gaming and gotta have the system? Nope.
I'm gonna wait til the first price drop. And if
that takes a year to happen then so be it. I'm
sooo tempted to go get one but my ethics keep my
money in my pocket. I'm not gonna give Sony $300
to play games and DVD's. Especially when I

already own a DVD player. I can't justify
spending that money. Realistically, the system,
plus memory card, one game and one controller
comes to approximately $453.97. Now to the
average consumer (mom and pop shopping on Xmas
for little Joey), that's a hefty price. A
Dreamcast with controller, memory card and game
comes to around $268.96. DO THE MATH! So next
year when the PS2 is finally down to around
$200.00 bucks, I'll get one. Unless I hit the
lottery or get my dream job before then. Or maybe
some Xmas money. So, until then I'm gonna spend
all my money on Shenmue, Jet Grind Radio, NBA2K1
and a slew of other DC games.

As always, thank you for jumping to vgt.com.

Torrence Davis

Editor In Chief

Start A Blog

To blog or not to blog, that is the question. Let me tell you something about blogging. Without blogging, a lot of us would have never made it in journalism. Before the Internet, you had to get a degree in journalism and then get a job at a newspaper or magazine to have a career as a journalist. If you wanted to self publish back then, you were literally printing your own newsletter and handing it out to friends and colleagues. That's great practice, but it wasn't going to secure you that big job at Time Magazine. If you self published a hardcover book, you were going to pay an arm and a leg for printing costs and still had to work on getting distribution. The Internet has allowed us to self publish basically for free. Before I was creating websites, I published a magazine. It was the only way to self publish, so with some help I published that first and only issue of Video Game Time magazine. I couldn't afford to print another issue of VGT, so that second issue became the website. The world wide web saved VGT and kept it going for many years. The great thing about having a full color magazine is that the publishers took me seriously.

So I'm going to answer that question for you. YES, you need to start a blog. It is by

far the easiest way to get into this racket.
Wordpress is free, it doesn't take much skill to
learn and it's a gateway into the world of
blogging. Publishing on the internet also means
free distribution and marketing. These are
things you have to pay for if you publish a
magazine. Also, magazines are dependent on
advertising and subscriptions to pay the bills.
You have no bills as a blogger except web hosting
fees and a yearly renewal on your domain. Once
your blog is up and running, the world is yours!
You can create whatever content you like, but try
to be original! If you fall into the bucket of
doing the same thing that everyone else does, you
will go unnnoticed. If you're doing this for
yourself, that's fine I guess. I became a
journalist to talk about games and then turned
that into a website. My second website was
centered around educating gamers, which I still
do to this day. I became a journalist during a
time where you could probably count on two hands
the number of publications that existed. I had
to change with the times. I was also first
publishing on the web when there weren't that
many video game websites. If you are starting
today and you don't do something original, you
will easily get lost in the fray.

The great thing about being alive today is
that if you don't want to blog, you can create a
podcast or do videos. However, a blog is a great
gateway to those other forms of media. Once you
create your blog and get some fans, you'll
instantly have an audience for your podcast or
videos. If fans really like your writing,
there's a huge chance they'll love any content
you put out. Keep that in mind as it is the
natural progression of a blogger these days.
Don't be afraid to write, talk and pose for the
camera. Come to think of it, doing videos is a
combination of writing and talking. Once you
master the writing and talking parts, videos
should be very easy to do.

When you finally get your blog up and running, wear that title on your chest! There's nothing wrong with being a blogger. Some paper journalists look down on bloggers. It's probably because they had to work much harder to become a journalist and bloggers are stealing food off their plates. Print is a dying format. If paper journalists don't know anything about blogging, they will die with the format. But seriously, what is blogging? It's writing content on the world wide web. Paper journalists can be bloggers and bloggers can be journalists. In fact, they are really one in the same. A lot of the people I work with in the gaming industry used to hate being called a journalist. They used to say, "I'm not a journalist, I just write about games". They don't want to wear the title because they think it's too pretentious. It is what it is. If you write about sports, you're a sports journalist. If you right about politics, you're a political journalist. If you write about games, you're a games journalist.

PR And How I Dealt With Them

Over the years of writing the magazine and building gaming websites, there was something that was always consistent…PR communications. In order to be a successful games journalist, you need to know how to deal with them. There are all kinds of PR reps in gaming and I'm going to try my best to talk about them all to give you the full spectrum on what you might expect. What you must understand is that they need you more than you need them. Back in 1995 it was a completely different game. Everything was print! When you are working in print you have two things, lead time and a deadline. The lead time is the window of time you have to complete your issue. The end of that lead time is your deadline. If you don't make the deadline, your story gets pushed to the next issue. At least that's how I would run things. You needed at least a month and a half to two months lead time to put an issue of your magazine together. That means for instance, if you were working on an issue that was to be published in April, you had to start putting it together in February. That's how long it would take you to get your info or review materials, play the games, grab screenshots, write your copy, layout your magazine, export a 4 color processed file, get film produced, take film to printer, check registration, print magazine and ship copies to stores and subscribers. Isn't that insane? That's exactly what I did for the first and only copy of Video Game Time magazine. It was a learning process but it was fun! In the process of creating this magazine, I had to make several calls to public relations representatives to get the very first thing I needed…review materials.

In order to procure review materials, you have to be professional. You don't just contact a PR person out of the blue and ask, "Hey can you send me a copy of Super Nuts 2"? There's certain tact that must be used. What I did first was establish a relationship with all the major PR reps. I had to call each publisher and ask who their press contact was. I got a full list of names, phone numbers and fax numbers. As I mentioned earlier, I faxed out a mission statement and details about my magazine *first*. This meant that when I called them to ask for preview or review copies, they knew who I was. It wasn't all business conversation either. These reps liked the fact that a fresh new publication wanted to talk about their games. They were interested to see what VGT was all about and what VGT was going to do for them. After establishing some communication and actually getting the goods, I had to make sure the work was done and the ROMS(Read Only Memory) were sent back in a decent amount of time. ROMs were basically cartridges before they went into production. Think of a Sega Genesis cartridge without the plastic casing. That was a ROM. A ROM was also an incomplete version of the game. If you lost it or didn't send it back, publishers were not going to be happy with you and would instantly write you off.

Jay Malpas from Data East sent me my very first SNES(Super Nintendo System) ROM to preview. I don't remember how I found it, but I managed to buy a video capture card for my PC. I hooked it up to my SNES and was able to quickly capture

screen shots of any game I played. After I
played a little and got my screen shots, I sent
the ROM back to Jay at Data East. This
established *trust.* Upon return recipe of the
ROM, I gained the publishers trust. I did this
with several other publishers like Working
Designs, Readysoft, Sunsoft, Capcom and many
others. After things started rolling I sweetened
the pot by giving my favorite publishers some
free ad space in my first issue of VGT. I needed
ads for the inside front cover and the inside and
outside back cover. ReadySoft and Data East
loved the idea and sent me film for full page
ads. It was great for them to not have to spend
money on ads and at the same time it made my
first issue of VGT look very professional!

After establishing these relationships, it
made it easier for me to get what I wanted. When
my first issue of VGT was published, I was sent a
Sega Saturn from Chris Kingry over at Sega. When
I went to E3 that year, I came home with all the
launch titles. Jay Malpas at Data East fulfilled
every request I sent him. ReadySoft sent me
every title they made. Alicia Kim was my contact
at Capcom for years! She was always very
helpful. The list goes on and on. In fact, some
of those relationships I created back in 1995
still exist to this day. Through these
relationships, I was able to get free consoles
from Panasonic, Negeo, Nintendo, Microsoft and
Sony. I'll never forget what they did for me,
but I'm still waiting for my Halo 3 duffel bag
from Microsoft and the highly coveted black PS1
from Sony.

Today is a bit different than back in 1995.
Today, most communication is done through email
or web forms. I can't remember the last time
I've actually talked to a PR rep on the phone.
Everything that I've procured for editorial
purposes since 2008 has been done through email.
It's easy and cuts out all the bullshit.
However, if I hadn't established a relationship

with the publisher, I had to prove myself worthy
of their press credentials. This meant sending
traffic reports, Alexa rankings and a sample of
my blood. Capcom had a simple setup that allowed
you to send a request via a form on their press
site. A lot of publishers adopted a press email
account for all of their requests. For instance,
if I wanted a game from Sega, I could send an
email to PR@sega.com and maybe they'll just send
the game…or not! Maybe they won't even respond
with a "no". Sometimes you'll be left in the
lurch and never hear from anyone. At other times,
you'll get a nice response asking for your
address or confirming that you will receive a
copy. It's somewhat of a game and each time you
have to roll the dice. What's crazy is that
sometimes a publisher will send you a game and
other times will not. Did they not like the
coverage of the last game they sent me? Maybe
they ran out of copies. It's always nice when
there's no copies to be sent and they actually
take the time to tell you.

One of the coolest relationships I had was
with Nick Jones of Shiny Entertainment. We
talked on the phone many times while he was
working on Earthworm Jim for Sega CD. They were
a couple hours north of where I was at the time,
but I never went to their office. Nick was cool
as shit though. He sent me a copy of EWJ(Earth
Worm Jim) CD right off the gold press. I still
have that copy today. This relationship with
Shiny Entertainment is what got me into the
Playboy Mansion. Another relationship I remember
was with BlueSky Software. These were the guys
who made Vectorman and many other sports and
platform titles. I got a call one day from them
to come out to the office to see Vectorman for
the first time. They were located in San Diego,
which is where I lived at the time, so it was
only a 20 minute drive to their office. When I
walked in I was blown away. The office cubicles
were filled with action figures, video game

paraphernalia and movie posters. One of the guys
was a kung fu movie nut like me. We hit it off
right away. We talked Jackie Chan and Shaw Bros
movies. I got to play Vectorman before anyone
else in the press. The game was amazing for it's
time. I don't even remember writing a story for
it at the time, but I think we published an
interview about Vectorman 2 at a later date.
Here's the interview ripped right off VGT.com
from the Internet archives.

We somehow got into bed with 3DO at the
time. They sent us a 3DO system and a bunch of
games. Naughty Dog was based in their apartment
in Cambridge, Massachusetts at the time. Guess
who lived in Cambridge? My Senior Editor and
cousin that I started it all with, Perry Mercer.
I made a phone call and he setup the interview.
He interviewed Jason Rubin and Andy Gavin in
their apartment. They were putting the finishing
touches on Way Of The Warrior and working on a
secret game for the Playstation which later
became Crash Bandicoot.

Dealing with PR can be somewhat of a skill
that you'll have to perfect. I'd say it's one of
the most important things to learn, even before
learning how to write. If you run your site and
can't write for shit, well at least you can get
your staff some games. It's all about synergy
though. You DO have to learn how to write, edit
and communicate well to make it in this business.
Oh and you have to have personality.

Secret PR Tips

1.
2. Sometimes you may have more than one PR contact at a publisher. When you request games, BCC all your contacts and you might get more than one copy of a game. This means you can have an extra copy to give away or keep for yourself.
3. A good choice of words to use when requesting review copies is, "Do you have any copies of Mega Missiles available for review?". It sounds less demanding than, "Can you send me a review copy of Mega Missiles?".
4. When you go to an event, ALWAYS introduce yourself to your PR contact. Smile and give them a good handshake! It's professional and face time is essential. Remember, these are the people sending you games and getting you into events. It's ok to kiss their ass.
5. If you are really interested in reviewing an upcoming game, let the PR rep know how much you love the game. If they think you'll give it a good review, they'll send it!
6. It's always cheaper for the publisher to send you a code than a physical game. ALWAYS ask for codes first!
7. Never ask for the super deluxe version of a game. One time Activision screwed up and sent us the Call Of Duty version with the

remote control car. It was supposed to be
sent to another outlet but I think they
switched our addresses…or maybe they meant
to send it?

8. Don't be afraid to ask for DLC codes! I
don't like paying for shitty DLC, but I have
no problem asking for it for free and
talking about it.

How To Junket

So what's a junket? A junket is when a publisher buys you a plane ticket, feeds you and puts you up in a hotel just to see their new game. Junkets are super fun because these publishers are willing to bend over backwards just so you can see their game, but the reality is that they want you to say good things about it. The idea is that if the publisher treats you really, really good, you'll have nothing bad to say about their game. To combat this, a lot of outlets will pay for their own travel accommodations. Sometimes just getting an invite is all they want or need. I've always run small outlets with no money. Yeah, we'd get an occasional ad buy and I could afford to buy food for the crew, but that's about it. So if a publisher offered to fly me or one of my crew out to an event, I had no issue with it.

I mentioned earlier in this book how we've been flown out to many events. Some of them were close to home and required me to drive like the Playboy Mansion event. Others were last minute all expenses paid "vacation junkets". Some were just trips into LA for one night to check out the release of a new game like Call Of Duty. Junkets are a great perk to being in this industry. There are however, people who frown on them because of the perception that the press is being "bought". Yeah, I had steak and lobster at the Jimmie Johnson event in Vegas, but I paid for my hotel room because I was invited late. On top of that, the game was fun.

So how do you junket? Well, if you're invited to a press junket, I'm sure you'll accept the invite, go over your itinerary with your PR contact, fly in, wine and dine, wake up and spend the day previewing a new game and then fly your ass back home. That's a junket in a nutshell. But how do you do it right? Well first off, you'll usually know what game you are going to be checking out before you get there. Make plans for content! If a publisher is willing to go through all of this to get you to check out their game, then plan ahead of time. Take pictures and maybe video at the venue, do an interview with a developer, play the game and write the preview. That right there is 4 or 5 posts for your site. Now you're ready for review copy right? Also, if you're the Editor In Chief, make sure the person who went to the junket is also the one who will be doing the review. They'll know more about the game than any other person you might have staffed on the site. That's working smart, not hard.

What do you do if you know there's a junket happening, but you weren't invited? Maybe you want to go and cover the event. First thing's first, send an email to your contact and politely ask them if they have room for you at their upcoming event. You could say, "Hello Mr. PR. Do you have anymore spots available at your Space Denizens event? I'd love to check out the game and write a preview. Thanks for your support!". This is actually how I got into the Call Of Duty XP event. Call Of Duty XP was probably the biggest event put on by a publisher. Activision invited press and celebrities to the event. If you weren't press, you could pay money to get into the event but they had limited tickets. I knew the event was coming and found out press were getting invites. I emailed Steve Cherrier at Activision and he hooked me up.

Speaking of Call Of Duty XP, it was one crazy event. It was like the grand daddy of every junket and party I'd ever been to. During the event, I ran into Xzibit and his son. This was odd because I also saw him at the San Diego Comic Con twice. First at the convention center and second at the Gaslamp District just chillin. I also ran into Kadeem Hardison on this Jeep experience they had. They drove us through mud and dirt and led us through a movie like gun fight through this building. That was pretty cool but it was even cooler that Kadeem was there the whole time. It had been the second time I had seen him at a gaming event. The other was an E3 party for gamers of color. I would later meet him a third time at another party not too long ago at E3. This time we conversed and took pictures together. There were other celebrities at Call Of Duty XP like William Fichtner, Nick Swardson and Chris Bosh. Kanye West had a full concert at the event and then showed up at the after party later that night. Not unlike Ice-T at Sega's party many years ago, Kanye walked right past me…trying his hardest to look hard. It was comical. Dude just looked angry. They actually kicked us out of a booth so him and his dancers could chill. In the adjacent booth was none other than Robert Kotick who was sitting with Terri Hatcher. I was thinking to myself, "WTF is Terri Hatcher doing hanging with Bobby Kotick?!!?". She looked like she was having a good time just yamming it up with him too!

So yeah, have fun at junkets but make sure you come back with a story. Also, don't worry about spending the publisher's money. They want you to, so just take the ticket and the hotel and create some history for yourself.

The Interview

Interviewing is the process of asking questions to the interviewee in order to extract information for an article or report. Good interviewing takes skill and good interviewers get the best scoops. I used to love getting the opportunity to interview a developer. I could ask those questions that no one had answers to and publish some fresh new content. The great thing about interviewing is the fact that you could get a scoop that no one else had. With a press release or a trailer drop, everyone is getting the same info and it's up to the writer to editorialize the info to give a unique perspective. Things were slower back in the early days of print and even the world wide web. If you got the chance to interview a developer, it was huge! It was like you were being allowed into the lab to get a taste of what was eventually going to be on gamers' screens all over the world. It was something special and when we got that opportunity, it was also a chance to build a direct relationship with the developer.

I had tight relationships with BlueSky Software, Madcatz, Shiny Entertainment and Psygnosis. This allowed me to get inside scoops on things before other outlets could. Perry scored that awesome interview with Naughty Dog in their apartment in Cambridge and also scored some great opportunities with Psygnosis due to the relationship that I had built with them. As of this writing, Madcatz has filed for Bankruptcy bringing an end to an almost 18 year relationship. That's crazy if you think about it.

So as I made the transformation from written interviews into video interviews, I noticed that the work I was doing was redundant. Developers didn't want to answer the tough questions because they had to follow certain protocols from the publisher. So the standard questions always came up every time. I'd ask them things like, "How long have you been working on this game?", "Will there be any DLC?" and "What were some of your influences?" Boring right? I started changing it up by not even asking about the game they were working on. I'd ask them about what games they were currently playing, what their favorite console was and how long they've been developing games. It made it more interesting, but because I really couldn't get the nitty and the gritty from them, I just got sick of doing interviews. That's not to say that interviewing isn't a great way to get fresh content on your site. Take Hiphopgamer for instance. He's one of the most amped up interviewers that I know and he still loves to do it. If it's something that you want to do, then do it!

So what makes a good interviewer? Well first, find yourself. Figure out what you like and use that as a means to create a good interview. Remember when you weren't writing about video games and you would read other interviews in the hopes the interviewer would ask specific questions but didn't? Well ask those questions. It helps to write down your questions ahead of time so you don't get stuck thinking about what to ask next. If you are doing a written interview you don't have as much pressure for time, but if you are doing a video interview, it's gotta go smooth. Also, video interviews should be short and sweet. No developer wants to stand there for 30 minutes answering questions. However, if you meet a developer for lunch or at a hotel in a relaxed environment, you might get that extra time you need. That's why those situations work better for written interviews than they do for video interviews. Most of my video interviews were at press events with hundreds of other journalists looking to do interviews too. This meant I had to sometimes wait in line to get some camera time with them.

There have been many times where I ran into developers at E3 on the show floor. Let me tell you something, if you ever see a developer on the show floor or walking somewhere, do not hesitate to stop them and politely ask them one or two questions. I ran into a SquareEnix developer who was working on FFXV many moons ago. Back then it was called Final Fantasy Versus and was exclusive to the Playstion 3. I asked him if it was coming out on Xbox and he told me that they were considering it. Several years later after a title change, the game arrived on Playstation 4 and Xbox One. That's called getting a scoop! I remember hearing about GTAV being in the early game play testing stages by overhearing a conversation at Valve's meeting room at E3. The stuff you find out if you have your ears and eyes open can be really interesting.

Select Interviews From The Past

Interview with BlueSky Software(1997)

We've been keeping up with the Vectorman 2 development since April of this year. Now that the game is finally finished, we decided to talk to the programmers and get their input on game development.

VGT: How long has Vectorman 2 been in development?

BS: **It was an 8 month development time**

VGT: When will the final release date be?

BS: **November 2**

VGT: Will this be Bluesky's last 16-bit title or will you continue to produce 16-bit titles?

BS: **To my knowledge this is the last 16-bit title**

VGT: Do you plan on moving Vectorman to 32-bit?

BS: I don't think there's any question that we wouldn't mind doing that, it's a question of the fact that we have to have a deal in place. It has to be a good enough deal to benefit Bluesky, and one that looks good for Vectorman. It would be great to move Vectorman to a 32-bit platform or even a PC. You have essentially unlimited memory and a lot more processing power. We did produce a design for a Saturn game. Were it goes from there we're not exactly sure.

VGT: As far as the Vectorman movie goes, will you guys have any creative control?

BS: John Shapiro was down last Friday and was very please at the amount of stuff that we had here. They're already at an advanced stage of writing a script, but they were really pleased at what they were able to get from the game. and some other materials that Sega provided. Coming down here was a fun experience because they found they were on the mark in a lot of ways with what we felt about the character too. They want to work with us as much as they can, and as their schedule allows. We expressed to them that we'd like to help with the project as much as possible.

VGT: Is this going to be more like a Disney type Toy Story, or is it going to be a little more deep and hard-core?

BS: They gave us indication that it will be more deeper than a Toy Story treatment. They want it all to be 3D of course, and there will be some similarities in the two films in being totally PG enterprises, but they don't want that clean look that Disney gave Toy Story. They want it to be very much their own look and feel. It will come down to what studio produces the film, and what that studio brings to the table in terms of look and feel. Right now they don't know their budget, so it's all going to depend on how much they have to work with. They indicated that they wouldn't mind having a Xmas 97 release, which is really aggressive. At that time, they had inquires as to whether we were doing a 32-bit Vectorman. The opportunity to release the two products at the same time apparently would be nice, but even in the gaming industry, Xmas 97 right now is really aggressive.

VGT: What about the Nintendo 64? Will you get into that?

BS: A lot of people here would like to work on the Nintendo, but Nintendo has some unusual practices concerning who they'll let develop. At this time I don't believe we're getting into that.

VGT: How do you feel about the cartridge format VS CD's"

BS: Cartridges are limited. CD is slower but it's a lot more space. Cartridges are a very expensive dead-end product. Nintendo will make it work for a little while but they've gotta be planning a new replacement for it.

VGT: Now being programmer's, as far as development tools go, have the Saturn development tools gotten any better than they were a year ago. Is it easier to work with?

BS: Everything improves over time. Saturn and Playstation for that matter, will have better and better tools every year. They'll never equal the

PC just because of the number of people working on each platform.

VGT: Do you feel that if you come out with a game on both platforms, the games will be produced on the same level? Do you think one will have better speed, graphics, and texture maps?

BS: With the current level of PC hardware, the platforms will always be faster. PC's are catching up really fast thought. The base system right now is a Pentium 133. So right now they'll be pretty comparable.

VGT: As you get more used to the development tools, is development time longer or shorter?

BS: What happened with the Genesis is that after working with it for a couple of years, we really got good at it, and I think that's reflected in Vectorman 1 and 2. When the quality of the tools and engine go up, we put in more game. The game improves, our development time stays the same or gets longer. I don't see that changing. If you want a good game, you have to spend the time. From the art side, the more graphics you put in, the better your resolution, the more time you have to refine your graphics. You can have the best tools in the world but you still have to spend more time to do more levels.

VGT: Do you think that now that the N64 is out, more people will steer away from the 32-bit systems, or do you think it will stay the same?

BS: That's hard to tell. There's a lot of Nintendo loyalty out there. It's a really nice system, but they've only got two games, and I hear there's not going to be that many more games released before Xmas.

VGT: They said maybe 5 or 6 games before Xmas.

BS: Don't hold your breath.

VGT: What about game prices.

BS: They're expensive. If I can buy a game for the Playstation or Saturn for 30 bucks, you're going to really have to impress me to spend 80 bucks for the Nintendo games. Mario is a great game, but you can only play one game so much before you get bored with it, then you want something new. And how many of the Nintendo games are going to be on the Mario level quality as far as development? Most of us don't have that luxury of a two and a half year development cycle.

VGT: From a programming standpoint, what would you tell would-be programmers?

BS: Buy a computer and start programming it. Don't let anyone tell you that you can't do it. There are jobs in this industry that are hard to find but don't give up. Don't let your friends tell you you'll never be a video game programmer.

Naughty Dog Interview (May 1995)

Back in May I had a chance to interview Andy Gavin, one half of the team that makes up Naughty Dog Software. The other half consist of Jason Rubin who's a graphic arts specialist. These guys are based in Cambridge, MA., where I happen to be from, and have created what may be the best fighting game for the 3DO. I played Way of the Warrior and it definitely blows the first Mortal Kombat away easily. The game is similar to Mortal Kombat in many ways. The digitized characters, fatalities, combos, blood galore, hidden characters, and special attacks are all here. What Way of the Warrior does is take if a step further with an amazing AI(Artificial Intelligence), characters that shrink and grow, over 50 attack moves for each character, 100% 3D scrolling, hidden weapons, interactive backgrounds, bonus items, and so much more. Let's have a talk with Andy and see what he has to say about Way of the Warrior.

VGT: When did you first start programming video games?

Andy: About 1 0-12 years ago, the first game we made was Ski Craze on the Apple II, which came out in 1986. It sold a couple thousand copies. Dream Zone was our next game that sold about 15000 copies. Kief the Thief, from Electronic Arts, did much better and sold about 50,000 copies on various machines. We then did Rings of Power, which was our only Genesis cartridge. It's

was very complex and sophisticated and took about 2 1/2 years to produce.

VGT: When was Naughty Dog founded?

Andy: Well , Naughty consists of mainly Jason Rubin and myself . Naughty got its names from a cartoon character that Jason drew. (Andy showed me a picture of an old Naughty Dog logo). Their new logo is on their flyers. The character was created about 8 years ago.

VGT: Is there any downside when programming on the 3DO with their CO's? Does access time and RAM space affect your games?

Andy: Well, first of all the 3DO has 3 megabytes, not mega bits of RAM, which is bigger then the largest SNES cartridge. The CD itself is 660 megabytes . There are technical issues that need to be addressed when programming on the 3DO. One has to use clever designs to reduce and eliminate load times. In Way of the Warrior the entire program was designed in what we call, Asynchronous. The loading is done while you play, by anticipating what needs to be loaded' in advance with a hardware process called DMA(Direct Memory Access) . There 's a short pause going into a fight, but once the action has begun, there is no pause. Players can perform all their moves, with fatalities, 3D scrolling and the stereo music blaring, but with no load time.

VGT: So even though we're playing continuously, there's no slow down what's so ever.

Andy: Yes, the 3DO is capable of loading stuff without any slow down. However, many previous CD games, including the 3DO, have had notable slow delays.

VGT: Like the Sega CD for instance?

Andy: Yes, this is due to sloppy, programming and not being aware of how to program on CD's. It's a difficult issue when writing programs that can actually play and load at the same time. It's a technical challenge. With good program design the load time can be minimized. In turn, the quality of the sound effect, music, FMV, and game play surpass any cartridge game. Cartridge games only have a limited amount of memory in which you can program. CD's only cost a dollar to manufacture, while cartridges can cost anywhere from 20-30 dollars. CD's have enormously superior cost to storage ratio.

VGT: Can the access time for the Sega CD be reduced with technical design programming?

Andy: They can definitely reduce the access time. I don't know that much about the Sega CD though. I don't think their DMA is better than the 3DO. The 3DO has 4-5 times more memory. It also has a CD drive that's twice as fast. It has decompression hardware that effectively doubles the speed. It has a unique and extremely powerful custom DMA architecture that can move graphics from disk to memory to screen and back without effecting game play.

VGT: What makes Way of the Warrior different from all the other fighting games?

Andy: As I mentioned before, I have an Artificial Intelligence Graduate degree from MIT. The computer players in WOTW are much more sophisticated then in other fighting games. Whereas they often resorted to patterns to beat the human players, there are no patterns programmed in for WOTW. It uses research grade AI

that learns the best way to beat you. It's
extremely cunning and different and actually
looks like a real player fighting by adapting to
the situation and using all it's moves.

VGT: Is it always learning consistently more and
more each time you play it?

Andy: Yes.

VGT: What about the characters? What makes them
so special.

**Andy: The characters have around 50 normal moves
and about 15-20 special moves. These moves
reflect their styles and personalities. There are
many secrets that use the background area and
hidden characters can also be found.**

VGT: So is each character equal in sense or are
some stronger then others?

**Andy: All the normal human characters are
designed to be equal even though they're
different.**

VGT: Well, I remember the first Street Fighter II
game had very uneven characters. Some had a major
advantage over others.

**Andy: It's tough to get the characters exactly
even. We tried to get them as close as possible.
People also developed different strategies for
beaten the other characters. There are a lot of
unique techniques and abilities for each
character. Like Konotori, which means "stork" in
Japanese, can flap and stay in the air longer.
Major Gaines has special steroids' implants that
can change his size and therefore the amount of
damage he receives become minimal. Nikki Chan is
a Chinese Kung Fu artist who can do flips with**

special moves. She's very fast and agile. Crimson Glory has close in grabs and special multi-missles that can be fired. Some character has special weapons. Nabu Naga has a sword and throwing stars. Shaky Jake has a staff.

VGT: There seems to be a little bit of everything from all the other fighting games in this game.

Andy: The other fighting games are very narrow. Most of them are to much alike. What we tried to do was take everything good from all the other fighting games and combine them all into WOTW. We've added unique features with better graphics, sounds, 3D backgrounds, special magic and potions, panning and zooming, background interaction, and larger more detailed characters.

VGT: Was the process of digitizing the characters the same as Mortal Kombat.

Andy: There are similarities. We've never seen them actually doing it. We have seen photos in magazines. They are actually a little more regimented then ours. Their fighting engine is much less sophisticated then WOFW. It requires that every characters moves line up to the exact same position. When each character does a high punch in Mortal Kombat, they high punch at the exact same point. So when they digitize their characters they have to line up perfectly. In WOTW, every character has its own information so not all characters need to have a high punch. Some of the characters punch high, some low, while others are tall, short, big and small. There's no requirement that the character be the same size. We built the character the same way the actor would appear, rather then force them to convert to our pre-requirements.

VGT: With the 3DO having such a small user base at this point, do you think it can increase sales and become successful?

Andy: We think it has a good chance. All game systems start off with a small user base. People forget the Genesis came out in August of 1989 and 2 years later when the Super Nintendo was released it only had 700,000 machines out there and only 23 games after the first year. 3DO already has more then that. The 3DO is the first of the 32/64bit machines and the difference is academic. Sony, Sega, and Nintendo have all announce 32/64bit systems that won't be available until 1995. The 3DO will be the only significant 32bit machine when Christmas comes. It will have a year of development by then and the price will probably drop some more. So I think it's in good shape. We hope WOTW with help sell systems.

VGT: Are there any other projects being worked on for the 3DO?

Andy: We have 2 other projects we're working on, but we can't comment on them at this point.

VGT: Do you think that CD's are the way to go for our future programmers?

Andy: I think this year is the year of the CD's. It already has the PC market. It offers so many advantages in cost and amount of storage . The access time disadvantage can be overcome with well-designed machines and good programming techniques.

VGT: Are there any other types of games that Naughty Dog will be working on besides fighting?

Andy: We signed a deal to put WOTW in the arcades.

VGT: If WOTW does come to the arcade, will it be different then the 3DO version.

Andy: It would be a bit different. The basis of it would be the same. There are different constraints for the arcade version. The 3DO is capable of producing arcade quality games.

VGT: What's the most outstanding achievement you've seen in video games today? What games really blow your mind?

Andy: I have favorites over the years. I tried Ridge Racer which was very impressive looking, but had mediocre game play. In the PC world, "DOOM!" was very good looking. It shows us that 3D games are here and can be produced very well, even on PC's.

VGT: Well, that's about it for the questions. Thank you very much for taking the time to be interviewed by VGT. We all hope that Way of the Warrior is very successful and we look forward to reviewing it and any other games that are produced by Naughty Dog.

Andy: Your welcome. Thank you for choosing Naughty Dog as your first interview. We look forward to reading VGT when it's released.

Special Thanks

My Dad for taking me to the MIT arcade.

My Mom for buying that copy of MS. Pac-Man.

My girlfriend Wendy for giving Call Of Duty a try, buying me my first Oculus AND editing this book for me!

My son Tevin for kicking my ass in UFC so much AND teaching me how to play Zombies.

My Aunt Lee for buying that copy of Pac-Man and sending it to me AND introducing me to PC Gaming.

My Aunt Romaine for never slapping me and playing shooters with me.

My cousin Perry for being my big brother and introducing me to every new game that came out AND being my Senior Editor for VGT.

My best friend Bubba for turning Space Invaders over 100's of times AND moving his foot which resetted the Apple II right after we found the idol in Aztec and were about to beat the game.

Matt for all those crazy nights playing FirePro Wrestling, retro gaming love AND being the first editor I hired for VGT.

Paul for reviewing all those games for VGT.

Joe for letting me CRITICAL him so many times in FirePro Wrestling.

Lee Yi, Hiphopgamer, Andrea Rene, Tony Polanco, Jorge Murphy, Art Lincoln, Aaron Greenberg, Eric Mudd, Anthony Canepa,Blaackstarr, Nelson Rodriguez, Alex Verrey, Michael Meyers, Wendy Spander, Ed Semrad, Dave Halverson, Dave Oshry, Juan Arriaga, SonyaWinz, Jeffrey Wilson, Nick Chester, Charles King, Chris Sealy, Dev Vaghela, Redinferno124 IXxICONxXI, Ajbreezy, Steven Thompson, ElricRepps, Randen Montalvo, John Noonan, Wessam Ibrahimovic, Tatjana Vejnovic, Maylene Garcia, Jack Hannikian, John Agan, Freddy Vasquez, Shinobi602, RubeninAZ, MikeMadden, Amir Miller, Daniel Lawson, Hayabusa90, Robert Workman, Ahsan Rasheed, Carlos Romero, Colton Dombrowski, Oscar Gonzalez, Randil Hines, Shannon Gerritzen, Zh1nt0, Jeff Rubenstein,Jim Redner, Andru Edwards, Zack Warren, Camile Warren, Jon Shaw, Tawanna Sharpe, Aisha Tyler, Raychul Moore, Aimee Lyn, Manny Lopez, Gary Swaby, Anthony Fraser, Brian Munjoma, BigLegendD, Michael Crawford, Andre Tipton, Anthony Severino, Da Commish, CtrlAltKill, Kapado, OOGFunk, DJ Killzownjones, Mario Pendleton, Nakai Willis,Kweku, WeaponX, Jagon, Atticus, Bret Murdock, Rachel Murdock, Patrick Seybold, Michelle Osorio, Stevie G, Gary Keith, Tom Carroll, Jennifer Fitzsimmons, Lesli Howard, Kelly Knight, Lisa Martinez, Matt Atwood, Howard Schwartz, Mark Day, Chris Kramer, Sean Mylett, Elizabeth Capps, Amy Rush, Alicia Peck, Christopher Kingry, Michael Latham, Andrea Vassallo, Jay Malpas, Gail Rubin, Carrie Tice, Kenji Yoshioka, Sandra Yee, Steve Crow, Nick Jones, David Perry, Marty Davis, Masumi Matsunaga, Sue Sesserman, Jeffrey Castaneda, Stacey Sujishi

89412357R00068

Made in the USA
Middletown, DE
16 September 2018